'Neath Verdun

'Neath Verdun

The experiences of a French soldier during
the early months of the First World War

Maurice Genevoix

Translated by H. Graham Richards

LEONAUR

'Neath Verdun
The experiences of a French soldier during
the early months of the First World War
by Maurice Genevoix
Translated by H. Graham Richards

First published under the title
'Neath Verdun

Leonaur is an imprint
of Oakpast Ltd

ISBN: 978-0-85706-208-6 (hardcover)
ISBN:978-0-85706-207-9 (softcover)

http://www.leonaur.com

Contents

DEDICATION

TO THE MEMORY OF MY FRIEND

ROBERT PORCHON

MENTIONED IN ARMY ORDERS FOR "ADMIRABLE BRAVERY"

KILLED AT LES EPARGES THE 20TH OF FEBRUARY, 1915

Prefatory Note

The following work had been scrutinized by the French Military Authorities, and the word (*Censored*) will be found in the text to indicate the eliminations they have deemed it expedient to make.

Preface

The author of this work, Mr. Maurice Genevoix, is a second-year student at the Ecole Normale, Paris (at the time of first publication). Having finished the second year of his course and, incidentally, completed a study "on Maupassant," he was in a position to regard with pleasant anticipation the vacation due to fall in July, 1914—a month later he received his baptism of fire, and of what a fire!

He supplies us with an invaluable picture of the war.

In the first place, the writer is endowed with astonishing powers of observation; he sees all in a glance, he hears everything. The intense power of concentration he possesses enables him instantly to seize upon all essentials of a particular incident or scene, and so to harmonize them as to produce a picture true to life.

Nothing escapes him—the song or hiss of bullets, the diverse notes of hurtling shells, the explosions, the shatterings—every tone of the infernal uproar; the breezes that pass, those that follow the explosions, those that have caressed the bodies of the dead "Whose frightful odour poisons the air;" the faces of men in moments of great crisis, their words, their dialogues; and, finally, the changing appearances of inanimate things, for are not actions for ever associated in the mind with the changing aspects of nature?

The pre-eminent, outstanding merit of the work, however, consists in the never failing sincerity of its author.

Many of those accounts already published—joyous greetings from the trenches, or light-hearted letters most carefully selected from among many thousands—due to many reasons, such as the precautions taken by the Censor; the reluctance among non-combatants to emphasize their own inaction and well-being by contrast with the suffering of others; a natural and universal desire to make the best of things; the very human habit of seeking to explain numerous and diverse manifestations by one simple idea, for example, to attribute every great event to the heroism of every man involved—a heroism without an end; and finally, the tone of the Press, the banality of its optimism—all these things contribute to present a picture of war softened and sweetened, abounding in "good times." Such travesty of the truth at once revolts and fills with indignation those who fight. A war such as this has proved to be merits at least that we should hear and face unflinchingly the truth of it in all its entirety.

The regiment is on the march; towards the close of day it passes through a village:

> The entrance to the village, which is indeed little more than a hamlet, was choked with carriages, with ploughs and horse-rakes, which had been drawn to one side. In silence we pass before the shattered houses. Nothing remains but the mere shells of walls and distorted chimneys still standing above the wrecked hearths. Some charred beams have rolled almost into the middle of the roadway; a large mechanical mowing-machine raises its broken shaft like a stump.
>
> The regiment defiles through the gloomy evening; our steps resound lugubriously and violate the surrounding desolation. In a short while, when the last section will have disappeared over the summit of the hill, the cold and silent night will descend again on the village, and peace shroud the poor, dead houses.

The regiment is on the march, and it is raining:

> Resignation indeed is difficult of attainment when one knows, as we do, the increase of our sufferings the rain involves: the heavy clothes; the coldness which penetrates with the water; the hardened leather of our boots; trousers flapping against the legs and hindering each stride; the linen at the bottom of the knapsack—that precious linen, to feel which against one's skin is a sheer delight—hopelessly stained, transformed little by little into a sodden mass on which papers and bottles of pickles have left their stain; the mud that spurts "into one's face and covers one's hands; the confused arrival; the night all too short for sleep passed beneath a coat that freezes instead of warming; the whole body stiff, joints without suppleness, painful; and the departure with boots of wood which crush the feet like the torture-shoe. Hard, indeed, is resignation!

But something turns up which makes the regiment forget the rain and its own sufferings. It passes between lines of strangely still bodies—and those are the bodies of Frenchmen, their brothers.

They seem attired all in new clothes, those still figures, so continuously has the unceasing rain poured down upon them. Their flesh is decomposed. Seeing them so darkened, with lips so swollen, some of the men exclaimed: 'Hullo! These are Turks!'

Their bodies had been "sloped backwards," facing the road, as though "to watch us pass." The Germans, retreating after the days of the Marne, indulged freely in the folly of arranging the bodies of their victims after this fashion. The officer himself was for a moment overcome by this horrifying spectacle, but:

Come! Head erect and fists clenched! No more of that weakness that a moment ago assailed me. We must look unmoved on these poor dead and seek from them the inspiration of hate. It was the Boche in his flight who dragged these sorry things to the side of the road, who arranged this horrid spectacle for our express benefit, and we must never rest until the brute has drunk our cup of vengeance to the dregs.

The regiment has come to war; night falls, a night towards the end of September:

The cold became intense . . . those wounded who had not yet been recovered moan and cry aloud in their sufferings and distress. . . . 'Are you going to let me die here? . . . Drink! . . . Ah! . . . Stretcher-bearers! . . .'

And the soldiers, hearing those agonized cries, but chained to their posts by the word of duty, groan in anguish: 'What are they fooling about, those stretcher-bearers? . . .'

(*Censored.*)

'They are like fleas—never to be found when one most wants them!' And the cries continue—voices soft and strained and weary from having called so often and long:

(*Censored.*)

'Mother! Oh! Mother!—Jeanne! . . . *P'tite* Jeanne! . . . Oh! say that you can hear me Jeanne! . . . I am thirsty . . . so thirsty! . .' The cries of others make one shudder. 'Still, I say I won't . . . I won't die here, my God! . . . Stretcher-bearers! . . . Stretcher-bearers! . . . You joint-shearers, carve me up! . . . Ah! . . .'

13

The advance of the regiment is checked. The enemy, following his early retreat, which at times assumed the appearance of a veritable rout, turned at bay. The section in command of our lieutenant dig a trench and pass forty hours in it. It has rained and it is still raining. A furious downpour is succeeded by a trickling stream which drips ceaselessly above their heads:

> Motionless, and packed tight together in cramped and painful attitudes, we shiver in silence. Our sodden clothes freeze our skin; our saturated caps bear down on our temples with slow and painful pressure. We raise our feet as high as we can before us, but often it occurs that our frozen fingers give way, letting our feet slip down into the muddy torrent rushing along the bottom of the trench. Already our knapsacks have slipped into the water, while the tails of our greatcoats trail in it.

So one night was passed—and then a second. The relief was due to arrive at any moment; but would it ever appear, that relief?

> As for myself, I no longer hoped for it. I had gone past caring. We had been there a long time. . . . No one will come. No one could possibly relieve us placed as we were, at the edge of this forest, in this trench, beneath this rain! Never again would we see houses with the lights glowing in the windows, never again see barns in which the well-packed hay never got wet. Nor ever again would we undress ourselves to rest our bodies and free them of this terrible iciness. . . .

Then comes the end of endurance and patience:—

> It is no longer worthwhile even to trouble oneself by hoping!

Heart-rending scenes these, are they not? Is it imperative that they should be discounted? It is conceivable they may upset, even disgust, the reader; but because they cause us pain we must not shrink from them, for it is precisely through the medium of that pain that we enter into intimate contact and communion with our soldiers; in compelling ourselves to contemplate these realities, however unpalatable they may be, we learn to accord our soldiers that recognition, that admiration, that pity which is their due!

Equally candid are his observations on the morale of the combatants. There are moments when they are demoralized, when they are afraid, yes, afraid! During a bombardment, for example:

> With bodies hunched together, heads hidden beneath knap-

sacks, muscles strained and contorted, agonizedly awaiting the nerve-shattering shock of the explosions.

One day the regiment just about to enter the firing- line encounters a column of wounded making for the clearing stations—a long column which seems unending, and:

It is as if, in merely showing themselves, with their wounds and their bloodstains, with their appearance of exhaustion and their masques of suffering, they had said to our men: See! It is a battle that is being waged! See what it has brought us. . . . Don't go on! And the men who were going forward looked upon them with faces anxious and troubled with dread, with eyes wide and fevered, in the grip of a moral tempest.

Is it necessary to record these weaknesses? It is, because they represent nothing but the truth, and it is natural that the living flesh should shrink, willing not to die. When Henry IV. was on the point of charging in battle his emotions so overcame him that he was compelled to dismount from his horse. But for a moment only. And then he charged! The enemy found it incredible that this man who hurled himself into the fight as recklessly as any mere carabineer could conceivably be the king of France himself. And Turenne, trembling in the face of peril, reprimanded his body, saying: *"Thou tremblest, carcass!"* After which he forced himself to go where he least wished to go. And so is it with our soldiers:

They are marching; each step they take brings them nearer that zone where Death reigns today, and still they march onwards. They go to enter that region of death, each with his living body; that body which, in the clutch of terror, performs involuntarily the motions of men fighting, eyes straight levelled, finger resting on rifle trigger; and that must continue as long as may be necessary notwithstanding the whistling bullets flying by unceasingly, bullets which often times embed themselves with a horrible, dread little noise, which makes one swiftly turn one's head as though to say: 'Hallo! Look!' And looking, they see a comrade crumple up and say to themselves: 'Soon perhaps it will be I; maybe in an hour or in a minute or even in this passing second, it will be my turn.' Then fear makes its kingdom of the living flesh. They are afraid; unquestionably they fear. But being afraid, they remain at their posts. And they fight the flesh, compel their bodies to obedience, because that is as it should be, and because, indeed, they are men!

Such is the truth, the reality, which truth and reality, far from depressing me, gives me strength. I see the soldier as he is, I know him as he is, I love and admire him with complete confidence!

This work of Genevoix glorifies our *poilu*: reveals him as a man, highly strung and impressionable, capable of panic—the work quotes instances of such panic—but, at the same time, patient despite his temperament, enduring well-nigh beyond the powers of human endurance; a grumbler against heaven and earth, desiring always to be able precisely to account for all things—in particular he wishes to know where he is going and why he is going!—A jester full of strange quips and cranks; but docile on the whole, loving those officers who show they care for him; familiar with those who permit it, with a familiarity purely deferential; in fine, possessed of attributes and virtues which defy precise definition, wholly admirable without the slightest consciousness of it.

On the 12th September, 1914, when Genevoix was perusing a notice attached to a wall, "printed in letters two hands high," announcing the victory of the Marne, he watched some soldiers approach to read the placard in their turn.

The faces of all of them were mud-stained and hairy to the very lips . . . for the most part they were infinitely wearied and miserable. Nevertheless, these were the men who had just fought with a courage and energy more than human; these were the men who had proved themselves stronger far than German shells and steel; these men were the conquerors. I should have liked to have told each one of them of the glow of affection which suddenly surged through me; affection for these men who have now won for themselves the admiration and respect of the whole world, who have sacrificed themselves without ever uttering the word 'sacrifice,' without seeming conscious of the sublimity of their own heroism!

The work is not altogether devoid of moments of gaiety; the conversation of the soldiers to which each contributes his particular patois; the distribution of rations to the various sections; the claims which rain down upon the corporal: "What—that sugar! Not a very fat lump, is it? Why, the pile you just handed the 3rd is almost double as much!" To which the corporal: "If you are not satisfied go and make your complaint to the Ministry!"; the cutting up of a quarter of beef by one, Martin, a miner from the North, armed with a knife "which had been given to him by a prisoner—a good enough piece of goods, too, which knife indeed has not its equal among the whole company for carving up a piece of tough meat"—and the task ended, a sufficiently difficult one, achieved as it were by the inch, Martin triumphant, proclaiming himself to be "Some Butcher."

Then there is that lunch which our lieutenant orders on pay-day: an omelette, never to be forgotten; a slice of juicy ham; most wonderful of jams; hunches large and thick from a loaf of fresh bread; afterwards a pipe, the blue, fragrant smoke of which drifts slowly up to the rafters above us. And following these wonders, the night passed in a bed, with real sheets and blankets upon it ! The memories of other nights are evoked—rough nights spent on heaps of stones in the fields, or on the debris of splintered trees which litter the woods, or amid the humidity and mud of the trenches, or the discomforting dryness of the stubble-fields—and now, to be covered from head to foot with bedclothes in a soft, real bed!

Not yet was our amazement exhausted . . . in vain we sought with every inch of our bodies for some hard spot, for some lurking corner which would hurt; but no spot or corner was there which was not soft and warm! . . . And we lapsed into bursts of laughter; we expressed our delight and enthusiasm in burlesque, in jokes, each one of which provoked fresh outbursts of laughter. . . . .

(*Censored.*)

We, that is to say Porchon and myself: Lieutenant Porchon and Lieutenant Genevoix.

There could be nothing more delightful than the comradeship existing between Genevoix of the Ecole Normale and the St. Cyrien, Porchon. They had been trained for widely different destinies, these two young men; the Ecole Normale on the one hand, Saint Cyr on the other! And if they both turned out to be excellent officers, with nothing to choose between them, that does not merely prove the value of the education obtained at the Ecole Normale. It proves something better and greater than that: the deep accord, the healthy unanimity which exists between French minds. So these two companions count the days gaily; they are young and they are French. . . . But Porchon is the gayer of the two; Genevoix envies him a little for his ready laughter, for the never failing and welcome good humour, to enter into the spirit of which, he says, "I compelled myself as though seeking the conquest of a virtue. . . ."

I like, too, the melancholy underlying this work. This war, foreseen and predicted, but whose horrors completely transcend the imagination, this retrograde movement towards the almost forgotten barbarity of a humanity we thought was marching towards new horizons, was there ever equal cause for human sadness? And there where the Germans, hailing from all parts of Germany, of all professions and creeds, steep themselves to satiation in joys purely cannibalistic, how shall a soldier of France control his tears, or rather how shall he find heart to weep? . . .

I am pleased, too, that those superb sentiments which sustain courage in moments of superhuman fatigue, which exalt amid perils and horrors, should be touched upon, however lightly, in the following pages. They dwell in the inmost heart of us all, hidden by that timidity, that exaggerated sense of shame, which prohibits us from revealing what is best and most sacred in ourselves. A few words alone suffice, like those written after a reunion of officers when a captain found himself in command of a corps, because:

> The Colonel had been wounded, the commander of the 1st Battalion also had been wounded, while the commanders of the 2nd and 3rd Battalions had been killed.
> From the expression of the faces about me, from the serenity reflected in each man's eyes, I gathered we were all ready to face the future whatsoever it might contain. . . . It almost seemed we leaned on one another for support, brothers by the common faith within us. A grace exalted and fortified us! . . .

And how many times does the word "*Patrie*" occur in these pages? Once only, as far as I can remember. Genevoix, idling about the trenches one day, heard the chime of distant bells drifting over the woodlands. The Germans in their trenches heard the bells, as did our men in theirs, but they bore not the same message for us as for them. To our soldiers they said:

> Hope, sons of France! I am quite near you, I, the voice of all those firesides you have left behind you. To each of you I bring a vision of that corner of the earth in which his heart is embowered. I am the heart of your homeland beating against your heart. Let confidence be always with you, sons of France, confidence and might always. I rhyme the immortal life of the

Patrie!

But to the Germans they said:

Madmen, who believe that France could die! Listen to me: above the little church, the fragments of whose stained-glass windows strew the flagstones, the steeple still stands erect. It is from there I come to you, gaily, mockingly. Through me the whole village defies you. I can see! . . . I can see! . . . Whatsoever you have done I can see. Whatsoever you may yet do, I also will see. And I fear you not at all. For I know the day will come when the weather-cock on the steeple, who stares unceasingly towards the far horizon, will look down upon your mad, despairing flight, while the bodies of your numberless dead lie thick over all the land.

Ernest Lavisse.

1

Contact is Established

Tuesday, August 25th,

The order for departure descended upon us like a thunderbolt: instantly, driven by the apprehension that something or other might ultimately be forgotten, there ensued a precipitate scurrying here, there, and everywhere throughout the town. Only with difficulty did I find the time even to warn those who are dear to me. The last inspection on the barrack-square was over. Out of the canteen, where I had gone to snatch a mouthful of food, I rushed, crossed the yard in a stride, and here you behold me, as erect and stiff as a ramrod, before files of men in blue coats and red trousers.

I was just in time: the general himself had already reached the right of my section. I stood with sword at the salute, my right hand grasping its hilt, my left kneading the greasy paper containing my recent purchase—a pennyworth of bread and a nameless pork confection, which perspired.

The General halts before me; young, well setup in his tunic, with a face refined and full of energy.

"Good luck to you. Lieutenant."

"Thanks, General."

"Here's my hand, Lieutenant."

Did I not know it ? I felt the sandwich being reduced to pulp in my own hand.

"Don't you feel excited, Lieutenant?"

A touch of *legerdemain* and my sword has passed into my left hand. I grip firmly the hand extended to me and answer loudly, distinctly, fairly meeting his eyes:

"No, General."

And that is a lie: I am highly excited. I should have been ashamed not to be. There were so many impressions, so many fleeting reflections to shake me from head to foot ! But I well understood that "Don't you feel excited?" of the General. I said "No:" I spoke the truth.

We were going to Troyes. So at least we were told. From Troyes, we were evidently to proceed straight to Mulliouse, to occupy and defend that captured town. This also we were told.

The prospect delighted me. To go to Alsace and remain there was certainly not so glorious as to have won our way there; but, at the same time, the prospect was not one to be despised.

We defiled through the town: roadways echoing, handkerchiefs waving, some laughter, some tears.

A mistake in the route cost us a few additional miles of measured tramping. Gradually the pace grew easier, for the oldest reservists, still plump, perspired freely, making no complaint, however.

We saw some of our wounded before the doorway of a large grey building. They held out at arm's length for our inspection spiked helmets and little round forage caps with red bands on a khaki ground.

"We also!" we cried. "We are going there, my friends!"

A young workgirl, fair and buxom, smiles upon me, displaying all her teeth. She has a small, well-poised head and inviting, ruddy cheeks. Her smile does me a world of good; for I am going to war; the morrow perhaps will see me in the thick of it!

The train, at last. A mere black line of gaping trucks with a few first-class carriages. Entraining is a big affair; the young major, a dark and energetic man, urges his horse from group to group, shouting directions and commands, A constant murmur arises from the onlookers. Why in the name of everything has he given the order for the little tricoloured flags, which a moment since were waving above the marching battalion, to be removed? . . .

Slowly we draw out of the station as the eventide descends. The sunset is sombre, dominated by monstrous clouds of purple and virgin gold.

Through the night rolls on the convoy. Our old captain of the 27th draws off his iron-plated boots and displays his socks, brilliantly yellow and quite new. We stretch ourselves, we groan, we snore. A pointsman, busy with his levers, cries out to us to ask whither we are bound:

"Troyes? What a joke! You are on your way to Verdun! . . ."

To believe everything one is told is the first illusion.

O sullen silence of night travelling! Our faces grow dull and lifeless in the indistinct light which filters doubtfully through the blue shade.

From time to time, perched high up on the embankment, we flash past vague figures silhouetted against the darkened heavens; they are sentries guarding the line. Suddenly long white pencils of light evolve majestically out of the night's blackness, chasing away the shadows.

Walls and station lamps announce Verdun. For a further three or four miles we run on. At one o'clock in the morning we find ourselves at Charny. Amid much confusion the sections fall in opposite the doors of the wagons, from which a heavy mist now slowly drifts. And heavy-footed and slowly we set out on the march.

Wednesday, August 26th,

At daybreak we pass through Bras. Before the country cottages are huge piles of manure from which a light steam rises. Cocks are a-crow; but man is still sleeping. We march and still march. Little by little, I become conscious that a rather fevered curiosity is spreading through the ranks.

We overtake a regiment of field artillery, drawn out in an interminable file, resting by the wayside. Gunners and drivers are alike asleep, overcome by fatigue, the former sprawled on the gun carriages, mouths wide open; the latter with their noses buried in the manes of their horses. They too sleep, poor beasts, with muzzles drooping and knees bent.

We pass by, the heavy, nailed boots of the men echoing loudly on the roadway. But the artillerymen do not hear us; they sleep too soundly for that. We even find it necessary to prod the horses before they will move aside to let us pass.

Crossing the Meuse, we encountered immense herds of cattle. They were divided into hundreds corralled at the water's edge in a smooth meadow. The brutes were lying on the brown earth, with their muzzles upraised in an ever-changing chorus of lowing. Cattlemen in red trousers kept placid watch over them.

Vachérauville. It is broad daylight. We have called a halt on a piece of uncultivated land on the side of a hill. I am still feeling dull and knocked up after the long night passed in the box-like carriage.

There are about a thousand of us altogether. The men, having piled arms and thrown themselves down on the ground, are sleeping, too tired even to ask questions. Indeed, the detachment commander himself appears to be ignorant as to our final destination. He is a dear old fellow in spectacles. I can just imagine him by his own fireside, his feet in slippers, poking away and smoking a big pipe. I shall never get used to seeing him on horseback!

That nuisance, L—— promoted medical officer, fusses about here and there, his tongue wagging ceaselessly:

What is this water? It's bad! Typhoid! Typhoid!—And where do you come from, young man? Have you any cartridges?—Give that horse something to drink!—This *chasseur* is ill.—You are ill, my friend!—Yes, yes. You are ill!—Just show me your tongue!— Ah, we must dose you. Yes!—Yes! What, not ill? No? Not ill? More's the pity! They should have taken away his spurs!

A lamenting voice rings out:

"Where's the officer! Where's the officer!"

An old woman hastens up, her cap all awry, her hands raised to the skies.

"What shall I do? They have taken away the canopy of my well to make a fire. Who is going to indemnify me for it ?...

Loss, damage, indemnity; words, alas, we are to hear often enough!

Midday. Conveyances are passing along the road at the foot of the hill: huge four-wheeled wains, each drawn by a thin, mangy horse. Wickerwork baskets, bales of household goods, rabbit hutches, have hastily been flung into them. On the top, mattresses, pillows, eiderdowns of a faded red have been piled. And on these are sitting women with backs hunched and bent, their clasped hands drooping over their knees, their eyes dull and blank. One cannot tell from their expressionless faces whether or not they are suffering. They seem to be immersed in reflections purely animal and without end. Here and there from amid this lamentable medley of goods protrude the heads of dirty-nosed urchins, with light hair tangled and matted. A few bellowing cows follow the wagon, dragging at the ropes by which they are tied, and lowing. An awkward youth with large hands and immense feet, whip in hand, drives them forward by kicking them lustily in the haunches.

Suddenly, cries and the rattle of triggers ring out. I turn swiftly to find thirty of our men deploying as skirmishers, facing the crest. Our old captain, red as a beetroot, his small scared eyes darting wildly round, shouts at the top of his voice:

"Look out! Look out! Rapid fire! ... upon the enemy approaching ... at 800 yards. ..."

What can all this mean? Have we been taken by surprise? I look about, but can perceive nothing, absolutely nothing to cause an alarm. Then I see J—— hurriedly whispering in the captain's ear. Over the latter's face there instantly spreads an expression of complete astonishment:

"Cease fire! At once! At once, I say!

J—— turns away convulsed, slyly indicating with his forefinger rows of corn-stacks aligning the crest of the hill!

On the road leading to the village, we pass people in detached groups, each of which becomes a hotbed of gossip. The latest arrivals are questioned avidly and insatiably:

"So there was a machine-gun in the church tower, was there? . . . How long did they continue firing on you? . . . Is it true that almost all the wounded were hit in the feet or legs?"

I approach one such gathering. In the centre are two stragglers: one is silent and sad-faced; the other orates with much gesticulation. There is a slight scar on his face, where the blood has dried and coagulated. And he displays a bullet embedded in the padding of his great coat, like a needle in a piece of cloth.

One encounters these stragglers constantly.

(*Censored.*)

They form an endless procession, dragging one leg after the other, their faces feverish, their hair long and their beards dirty.

And here are still more wagons packed with women and children, or with wounded men, some of whom sit gripping the sides with both hands, while others lie stretched full length on blood-stained straw. Ammunition wagons go by at a gallop, creating a terrible rattle; groups of dusty infantry tramp over the withered grass by the roadside.

And so the torrent, descending from the top of the hill over which the road vanishes into the distance, streams on towards the bottom of the valley where the village lies. Does it mean a panic, this? I ask myself. Certainly not! But if not, then why this feeling of depression, of which, do what I will, I cannot rid myself?

A Staff-officer has arrived. Our detachment commander turns pale with emotion merely at the sight of his badges. It quickly transpires that we are to turn back across the Meuse the way we came. I learn the news without surprise; I was certain that that stream of stragglers boded ill for us.

A long march lies before us, over a monotonous road destitute of trees. The sky is gloomy, obscured by rain clouds. Moreover the atmosphere is oppressive. We revisit Bras and Charny, then Marre and Chattancourt: which villages all resemble each other, with their low-built houses—presenting a colour-scheme of washed-out blue and dirty yellow. And always, at the very thresholds of the cottages, is the inevitable pile of manure, spreading every now and again right into the middle of the roadway.

Esnes is like Marre and Chattancourt. We are billeted there with a young woman who has the face of a toothless doll and legs without calves. In a dark corner of the room, I catch a glimpse of some strange person, fondling a child still in swaddling clothes. Like a shadow he vanishes as we enter.

From the open door I watch a soldier in shirt-sleeves, forearms bare, slaughtering a sheep lying with its legs tied to a gate. Each agonized convulsion of the poor beast makes me feel ill; it brings back to my mind the time when, in a slaughter-house, I plunged my leg into a bucket filled with warm blood, streaming in a flood from the severed neck of a slaughtered cow! . . .

The evening set in grey and depressing. Fine rain began to fall, saturating everything. I thought of my men trying to rest out in the fields, lying round their piled arms, and set out to see if I could find shelter for them.

It did not prove difficult, for there was scarcely a soldier in the whole village. I found a barn full of hay, and returned to the meadow well pleased with myself:

"Up, boys! Bring your arms, packs, and the whole bag of tricks! There is a roof with good hay beneath it for you over there!"

Through the night and a rain increasing in violence I lead a *cortège* of mute shades. Alas! we do not get far. For in the village I encounter my commander, striding up and down before the houses, making himself quite ill from anxiety. "About turn! Quick march!" The shades return to the marsh, still mute. I listen to the slush-slush of their heavy boots as they tramp through the puddles. Poor devils!

Returning I meet a few soldiers moving towards the cemetery with its congregation of tombs clustering round the little church. They are carrying a body wrapped in a flag on a stretcher. Then I recollect someone mentioned that a cavalryman had been killed earlier in the day by a stray bullet.

Sleeping quarters I found to consist of a shabby garret. Sleep was fitful at the best. All through the night the door slammed. Every time

I opened my eyes, I saw by the dim rays of a smoky lamp other eyes hidden in the shadow of caps. On one side of me, in an alcove similar to mine, a sick man, tortured by a sharp attack of rheumatism, kept constantly moaning and crying.

Dawn at last! I dress myself hastily, only too thankful to escape the oppressive atmosphere of this hovel. I long to breathe the fresh air, to open my lungs, to escape as far as possible from that bed, from those greasy bedclothes which have communicated their dampness to my skin, from the musty smell of cheese, skim milk and pig's-wash....

It is still raining. In the distant meadow I can see stacked rifles and sodden knapsacks; but not a man is afoot. So much the worse. . . Bravo!

Thursday, August 27th.

Another long march, protracted and dawdling. Indeed it could not justly be described as a march at all; rather was it the wandering of men who had lost their way. Haucourt, then Malancourt, then Béthincourt. The road is a mere river of mud. At each step a jet of yellow water spurts upwards. Heavier and heavier becomes my great coat. It is useless for me to bury my neck between my shoulders: large drops of cold rain contrive to work themselves inside my collar and trickle down my back. My knapsack bumps to and fro against my hips. Whenever a halt is called, I remain standing, not daring even to raise an arm lest the penalty be still more water down my back.

We find that we have arrived at Gercourt, which proves to be our immediate destination. A splash of blue breaks through the rain clouds. Our uniforms begin to recover their original colours, brass buttons to gleam.

The day's march is ended! I turn my back to the increasing warmth while trying to masticate a stringy piece of meat and some elastic-like bread. Above the men, standing easy, a mist of evaporating water rises and drifts away.

"All officers stand forward!"

Something apparently is about to occur. It turns out to be the adjutant coming to give instructions from the colonel. He is a big, dark, active man. He steps forward, drums beating: twelve files, one per company. Things move quickly for us too; a shower of questions descends upon us like an avalanche; there is no time to reply before it is all over. I am to join up with the 7th Company as the regiment passes.

My regiment arrives! Our reservists run as fast as they can towards the embanked roadway. And a fine medley ensues! Greetings shouted from afar; exclamations of pleasure exchanged between the marching files and the men gathered on the banks. There is anxiety in the eyes of almost everyone looking upon those who have already fought. Some of the men return to the stacked rifles with faces lowered and arms listlessly swinging.

I slip into my place as the 7th passes. And as the march proceeds the same questions are heard on every hand: "What about Robert?—He is wounded. A bullet in the shoulder. Not serious.—And Jean?—He is dead...."

It is the brother of those two soldiers, the one wounded, the other killed, who replies. He lets fall these words in a breathless voice as he runs to resume his place in the ranks.

We halt in column in a parched meadow. I take advantage of this opportunity to present myself to my captain. He is a big, finely-built man, with powerful body supported by rather slender legs. The quick and penetrating glance he gives me tends to weaken my first impression, which led me to regard him as being rather slow-witted.

"Ah, young man, so you are entering on your apprenticeship! You have come to a good school, as you will learn. A good school! "

A smile wrinkles the corners of his blue eyes. It would seem that my superior has a pronounced taste for irony!

There is also a second-lieutenant attached to my company, a Saint-Maixentian, young and solid, and something of a dandy. He has a flaming moustache rather too heavy for his ruddy, chubby face, possesses massive shoulders, thick wrists and calves. He puts out his hand and at once offers me a sip of gin as an appropriate prelude to further acquaintanceship.

"Wait a little, old man, and you shall see how we'll mop them up!"

He flings out an arm and with a sweep indicates the horizon and the village of Cuisy, which is close at hand.

Five minutes afterwards, the whole regiment descends a steep road between two high banks covered with bushes. The stones slip beneath our feet; we clutch one another; we snatch at branches for support; my sword becomes an alpenstock.

As soon as we get out into the country, we find ourselves once more in the mud and slush. We pass many barns but few houses. A village containing perhaps a hundred inhabitants is our resting-place. And there room must be found for three thousand of us. Let it be understood, we never would have occupied such a hole had there been no War!

It is night. I know that we are supposed to be messing with the officers of the 8th. But where? No one has mentioned a rendezvous. I remind myself that a campaigning soldier's first principle should be: "Rely upon thyself alone." And so, through the darkness and mud and inevitable manure, I set out to discover the mess.

The place of assembly is a dimly-lit kitchen. At one end, the yellow flame of a candle set the shadows dancing on the walls. A cook, bare of arms and grimy of paws, fingers and handles some meat as if he were kneading dough. A second, with a pipe between his teeth, skims the *pot-au-feu* whilst expectorating into the cinders. He raises towards me a face like that of a thick-lipped faun; his eyes are very clear, but unintelligent and slow-moving. The beginnings of a beard decorate his chin with a few odd hairs as stiff as bristles. It is he who receives me in a voice drawling and muffled—his mouth, it seems, is chock-full of macaroni.

One after the other the officers enter. There is the captain and the Saint-Maixentian, as well as a newly-commissioned cadet from Saint Cyr, bony of face, nose powerful, and altogether a good sort, I find, who, like myself, has just come from the depot. The captain of the 8th is a short, well-built, fair man, refined, meticulously well-groomed, with a smile that reveals his teeth, and a soft voice which he modulates beautifully. A lieutenant, powerfully built ... (*Censored.*) ... whose nose descends into his spoon ... (*Censored.*) ... regales us on vapid obscenities. Finally, there is a second-lieutenant, slender and delicate, dark, with a very boyish face, intelligent yet artless.

Dinner proceeds rather gloomily. The two captains exchange anecdotes concerning Morocco, or ready-made stories gleaned in the camps regarding fair women.

Once more I plunge through the mud. And I reflect that it would be foolish in the extreme not to profit by this stay in a village by trying to find a bed in which to pass the night. As a result, I ultimately slip between two crumpled sheets beside a farmer of fifty or so, who breathes heavily and smells strongly.

Nevertheless I sleep, and soundly too!

29

2

The Crossing of the Meuse

Friday, August 28th,
Four o'clock in the morning. We ascend to the top of a stony road. The night mists are still drifting. The whole regiment falls in near the village, in an orchard bounded by hedges. And there a monocled major in a sing-song voice reads aloud a stirring proclamation: it is the colonel's funeral oration, filled with vehement exhortations, and a poem of Déroulède's to finish up with. Much simpler and more touching is the sight of the soldiers presenting arms, and all the officers with their swords at the salute.

On the summit of a wind-swept crest, we dig trenches deep enough to accommodate men standing erect. I inhale the fresh air greedily, delighted to be out in the sunshine and happy, while my men dig away with their picks and throw shovelfuls of earth over the parapet.

An immense valley lies extended below us. At the foot of the hill are deeply shadowed woods interspersed with luminous lakes of well-mellowed crops. To the right, a road takes an abrupt turn and leads through an avenue of trees; in the foreground, a second road at right angles to the first, cuts an ugly gash through the dappled richness of the fields. At the bottom of the valley, the white walls of the village of Dannevoux peeps forth between the green leaves. And still further away, over towards the Meuse, invisible from this spot, is a chain of blue hills.

Until evening, the men dig with zest. From afar off sounds the muffled rumble of a violent cannonade. We take our lunch by the roadside, attacking a charred fowl with teeth and fingers, and drinking muddy wine to the last dregs. Tonight, as yesterday, I gratefully retire with my farmer; but on this occasion his snores haunt me, and he wakes me every time he moves.

Saturday, August 29th.

The men, with shirts opened and their skins wet with perspiration, complete their trenches beneath a searching and pitiless sun. Above the rumbling of distant artillery, we hear the detonations, still muffled and deadened, of nearer batteries. By holding my hand to my ear, I can distinguish soft whistlings which terminate in wailing explosions. Shrapnel evidently, the smoke of which is slowly dissipated in the calm air.

We retain our billets that night also, but not many of us sleep; for the German shells are bursting now hardly a mile away from the village; the windows shake and tremble under the stress of the formidable explosions.

Sunday, August 30th.

Bois de Septsarges. Hardy undergrowth thrusting forth roots shoots amid the shadows of the great forest. Great splashes of light are on the moss; living, quivering sun-rays pierce the warm gloom; the acrid odour of fermentation, increased by the sun, is oppressive. It strikes one forcibly, that sun! I recline in the shelter of a tree, moving only as the shade moves.

P———, a second-lieutenant of the 8th, lies weltering beside me. He is writing in pencil a long letter to his wife; he chats about her and his little girl, who is five months old. I pay him all the attention I possibly can, but I fear I do not understand much of what he says: his voice comes to me like a monotonous purring—which is, as it were, punctuated by the throbbing of the blood in my temples and fingers. And so I fall asleep.

A terrific explosion wakes me with a start. Three more successive detonations shatter the air, and above my head I hear the flight of shells—a light rustling, a rapid rushing, which one can with some difficult follow with the ear, growing more and more distant until it terminates finally in the explosion.

"Those are 120 mm. guns," P——— remarks to me.

Scarcely have the words crossed his lips before a succession of harsher and more violent explosions causes me to look away to the left. There is no hanging back for each other with these! They come altogether in a rush, yet each detonation is separately distinguishable, despite the deep murmur following the resounding, vibrating echo which steals through the undergrowth. I think a battery of our 75's must have urgent work on hand.

By the evening, the cannonade has become far heavier. The whistling shells pass and cross each other's course; the smaller ones furiously maintaining a flat trajectory; the bigger ones sailing past almost slowly, winging through the air with well-nigh dulcet tones. Quite mechanically I raise my eyes to watch them.

Every man hearing that noise for the first time, does the same thing.

When we leave the wood these "marmites" are bursting away to our left, near enough for us to hear, after the explosion, the hail of splinters striking the trees.

We remain in our billets as wakeful as on the preceding night, and this is to be my last night with my fat old man. Alas!

Monday, August 31st.

We set out for the Septsarges Wood again. The day is passed as was the preceding one. Grillon, a regimental barber, shaves me: a sensation which has already become strange to me. Two knapsacks for a stool, a tree for a backrest. I pay him with superfine tobacco, and he would have kissed me! I settle down again for a *siesta*, chasing the shade.

Towards two o'clock we make a fresh move. We push forward in a north-easterly direction, traversing the whole length of the wood until we reach trenches constructed by the engineers with a breastwork of tree-trunks in front. We take possession of them. A shelter made of branches is reserved for my occupation a little behind the line.

It would hardly have been natural had we not, in the course of our day's wanderings, received a few big Berthas—ten or so exploded in succession not thirty yards from us.

I passed the night in my bower. The branches of which it was constructed had become sun-dried and reminded me of the fact by affectionately digging me in the sides. My improvised mattress would not shake down properly, while the knapsack beneath my head acquired a sudden and spiteful hardness. I was not yet used to it.

Tuesday, September 1st.

We remain in the trenches. Some belated food is eagerly expected from the kitchen. Very shortly, however, the inevitable complete confusion descends upon us. For the fight is moving along to our front. The captain has sent word to say that the first line must have been broken through and that we must redouble our vigilance. Porchon, my Saint Cyrien, acting on orders, sends out a patrol away to the left. Hardly have they got clear when rifle shots ring out—we know well Lebels are speaking!—and the patrol tumbles back, scared. It appears they sighted the Boches and fired! My men become restless and anxious; there is a premonition of evil in the air.

Suddenly a shrill whistling bursts out and increases, increases ... until two shrapnel shells explode almost above my trench. I am down on the ground in a moment; and even in the act my attention is attracted and held by the terrified expression of one of the men. The memory of that man's face haunts me now!

Once again a messenger comes up at a run:

"The captain sends me to warn you that there is nothing now between you and the Germans!"

Is it true? We have seen the wounded coming down ... (*Censored*.) ...A corporal of the 27th, stained and perspiring, his face expressive of his agitation, calls out to inform me that Dalle-Leblane has a bullet through his stomach. Then a great tall fellow, shot through the thighs, goes by groaning. He raises both feet, resting the whole weight of his body on those supporting him. Good comrades those, and true heroes! They carefully set down the wounded man about ten yards from my trench and, having ridded themselves of their burden, make off. So it remains for me to have the man transported, still bellowing, to the battalion first-aid post.

The news reaches me, I know not by what means, that the —th are retiring, mainly on their left. It turns out to be true, for they come to relieve us, and we move back to new positions, five hundred yards to the rear.

Line in sections of fours, in a clearing. The shells begin to burst around us. At the very first explosion, a reservist, a big man, fair and ruddy, turns round sharply to tell me he is wounded. He is pale and trembling violently. I discover that he has been pricked by a thorn as he was bending down!

A second shell, and a street hawker from Ferrai is grasping a bleeding wrist. A third: Corporal Tremoult receives the end of someone else's rifle full in the mouth. For a moment he is dismayed; then, his spirit returning, he commences to swear to the point of extinction. This peppering continues.

Night. From afar sound the moans of the wounded. A mutilated horse whinnies in pain. Also there comes to my ears a strange and poignant lamentation—perhaps it is only the cry of a nightbird!

I make the round at eleven o'clock, crippled by the cold. Half an hour has passed since I called Porchon, but I am not yet asleep when the order for our withdrawal arrives. We return to the trenches at Cuisy.

Wednesday, September 2nd.

We have been here since two o'clock, and settle ourselves down with a curious sense of security and protection. Have they, the Boches, crossed the Meuse in number? Maybe! But, perched on the top of this elevation, we can await them tranquilly. Four days ago a machine-gunner came down to us with a range-finder and supplied me with exact ranges. Should they come, I shall be able to regulate our fire and we shall drive them down before they reach us.

Meanwhile we sleep. The stars are limpid and steady; the air freshens with the approach of day. Crouching right at the bottom of the trench on a bed of dry lucerne, I wrap myself tightly in my greatcoat and doze a little, a doze constantly broken by chill a wakings. At last my men, moving about me, succeed in rousing me. I rub my eyes, stretch my arms, and jump to my feet. The sun is rising and already floods the fields with a sea of soft light. I recognize my valley, with the range-points marked to the extreme limits of effective fire.

Many aeroplanes are up—ours bright and light, those of the Boches dark and sinister, but all of them dainty and with the calm unswerving flight of birds of prey.

One or two patrols of grey dragoons are scouting in a field of rye. A few shots coming from the right of us stop them. Before us at the edge of a wood is a *vedette* of *Uhlans*, horses and men quite motionless, except when, every now and again, one of the horses, fly-pestered, flicks its flanks with its tail.

Through my glasses, I distinguish two wounded men dragging themselves along a road—two Frenchmen. One of the *Uhlans* has also seen them. He has dismounted and is moving towards them. I follow the scene with concentrated attention. Now he is close to them and addresses them; then all three commence to move towards a thicket bordering the roadway, the German between the two Frenchmen, supporting them, without doubt encouraging them with words. And there, taking many precautions, the big, grey horseman helps our men to stretch themselves at ease. He leans over them and it is long before he rises; I am sure he is dressing their wounds! . . .

At two o'clock the shells come whistling over us again. A battery on the crest behind us has opened fire. The firing has endured for perhaps ten minutes or so, when suddenly a German shell bursts not ten yards in front of our trench. Quite automatically I raised my head the second following the explosion—and an invisible something passed growling beneath my very nose. A man near me says laughingly: "Mind the hornets! . . ." I have learnt a lesson. Good! The next time I won't get up before the swarm has passed. I have not long to wait. Four shells arrive at the same moment, then three more, then ten. This continues for almost an hour. We are all prone at the bottom of the trench, our bodies in the mud, our heads beneath our knapsacks. Between each outbreak of the tempest, the two men to the right of me labour feverishly to dig a *niche* for themselves in the trench side. They scratch away like a fox in the earth; I can see no more of them than the nails in their boots.

A dark, fantastically shaped, copper-coloured cloud of smoke, irritating throat and lungs, steals down upon us. It has not had time to clear before a fresh storm bursts. One can hear it approaching, irresistible; I feel the terrible shock as the first shell strikes the ground, before being deafened by the succeeding salvo.

During an interval of comparative calm, a noise of someone scrambling and sliding makes me quickly turn my head. One of my men has jumped out of the trench to the left and is running along the front of it towards the right, knapsack on back and rifle in hand, bayonet clinking, mess-tin rattling, cartridges shaking! The water-bottle on his hip beats a violent tattoo. He glares at me with eyes wild and dilated, and then hurls himself bodily back into the trench. Like a thunderbolt he falls right on top of his comrades before they can find time to jump aside. Much shouting and swearing ensues, punctuated by blows. A sudden squall of half a dozen high explosives serves, however, to restore peace among them. The shells fall uncomfortably near us, one indeed not more than five yards from me. For a moment it seemed as if the walls of earth had closed in upon me; a stone, several pounds in weight, catches me fair and square in the knapsack, driving my nose deeply into the clay and leaving me dazed for quite ten minutes.

The sunset is beautiful and soothing. Night falls clear and still. I walk up and down before the trench in a field of lucerne, stopping at the edges of the enormous craters dug by the shells, picking up here and there steel splinters, still warm, or copper fuses almost intact on which are inscribed numbers and abbreviated words. And then I return "home "and stretch myself out on the earth to sleep.

3

The Retreat

Thursday, September 3rd.

A messenger arouses me. The darkness of night is still with us. I consult my watch in the light of a match: it is only two o'clock! I feel convinced at once that we are going to attack. On a projecting stone the cook has placed my coffee. I drink it in one gulp; it is stone-cold, certainly, but that does not matter very much.

Where are we going? To Septsarges? I believe that must be our destination, until suddenly we branch off the road to the right and head directly for Montfaucon. Already the village appears before us, lining the side of a hill the summit of which is crowned with a church. I can now distinguish with the naked eye the red cross on the white flag floating above the hospital. At the foot of the hill we swing away to the left in a south-easterly direction. It is not to be Montfaucon after all!

For good reason too! Several regiments, the whole division in fact, is under orders to assemble in a ravine situated a few hundred yards from the village. The concentration, however, does not proceed rapidly.

(Censored.)

My company, as rearguard, is drawn up at the roadside. It is broad daylight now. How long are we destined to remain here? It was only yesterday we were bombarded at Cuisy!

I identify a distant explosion as emanating from the heavy German artillery. Is the compliment directed to us? The hiss teaches me that the shell is coming directly for us. Instinctively I look towards Montfaucon and see flames and dense smoke spurt out quite close to the church: two seconds elapse before the noise of the explosion reaches us.

That was the signal for pandemonium; shells shrieking, hissing, bursting; tiles falling in showers, walls smashing and crashing to the ground. The earth beneath my feet heaves and trembles; my very skin seems to ripple with the force of the outburst. I no longer know where I am. With a heavy heart I watch the plumes of smoke, black, red and yellow, arising on every side to mingle and form an enormous cloud, ominous, outrageous, drifting above the stricken village.

Ambulance cars with their sad burdens pass; burdens many of whom are very near the portals of death.

Wounded men follow on foot, some of whom are half lying on their crutches, others supporting the whole of their weight on two sticks. A chaplain is with them: he jests and smiles in an attempt to renew their confidence and courage.

An old man and his wife pass by, a piteous sight. The man carries on his back a huge basket full to overflowing; the old woman is bearing other napkin-covered baskets, one on each arm. They walk quickly, their eyes full of distress and fear; and they look back again and again towards their house from which they have been driven forth—their house which by this time, maybe, is no more than a smoking pile of ruins!

Across the meadows strides a farm labourer whose legs are obviously far too long for his body. He is shouting aloud and driving before him ten or more black and white cows. His enormous feet assist him in the task; beneath his cap one detects the malformed head of a *crétin*.

The column is far enough ahead by this time to permit us in our turn to take up the march. I can still distinguish, far away down the road, the old couple of a short while since—the woman appearing thin and diminutive between her two big baskets, while the old man's basket seems to be trotting along on two ridiculously small and inadequate legs. Behind us, the shells thunder down unceasingly upon Montfaucon.

We march, urged onwards by an indescribable cloud of dust. We are full of high spirits and completely confident that when the time comes we shall give a good account of ourselves; nevertheless, we cannot refrain from wonderingly asking ourselves where are our guns which should be able to silence those of the enemy? Apparently we are being out-manoeuvred; most obviously we are falling back. A certain thought hammers away at my brain until it dominates everything else; it is that we are but straws in the pathway of an overwhelming force!

37

Only yesterday in the trenches at Cuisy I was watching the German motorcars rushing on the roads in the plain which had just been a battlefield. The stretcher-bearers, too, were busy collecting the dead and wounded, and over towards Dannevoux the smoke of a fire mounted above the trees—the fire in which they were already cremating their dead. Their aeroplanes floated over our positions, signalling ranges and directions to their gunners. A *vedette* of cavalrymen acted as observers, defying fatigue, while patrol after patrol came through the fields of wheat and rye.

I pondered these things on this morning, and began to understand how tremendous was the organization which went to create this seemingly irresistible power.

I recalled also how only yesterday I had seen a battalion of Germans assemble between two woods scarcely two miles from our lines. The men had flung aside their coats and commenced, quite unperturbed, to dig trenches, while beside them the smoke of their camp kitchens rose in the air. And I had asked myself then with ever increasing amazement why our so greatly vaunted 75's did not drop a handful of shells in the middle of this group of Boches?

The road is dusty, our throats parched, our feet painful. Passing through Malancourt, which we have already visited once, then Avocourt, we reach the forest of Hesse. At the edge of a ditch lie some mutilated horses, their large eyes filmed and staring, their legs stiff. A white horse, just at the point of death, heavily raises its head and watches us pass. A charitable sergeant sends a bullet through its skull to put a term to its misery; the head sinks, the sides quiver with the last fluttering sigh.

The heat increases steadily. Stragglers line the road, sprawled full length in the strip of shade which edges the woods. Some fall out of the ranks, seat themselves phlegmatically, draw out some bread and corned beef, and placidly commence to eat.

Parois. The slaughter-houses of the Army Corps are here. The blood which has formed miniature lakes in front of the barns dries in the sun, filling the atmosphere with a sickening smell with which mingles the more powerful fumes of iodoform.

A long halt near Brabant, at the bottom of an airless declivity in which one perspires as in a bath. My mouth is burningly dry, I am fevered. I find it impossible to swallow a single mouthful; worse still I find sleep equally impossible.

By the time we reach Bracourt, lights are dancing before my eyes, a strange buzzing is in my ears. I let myself fall on to some straw, my limbs helpless, my head empty as a bell, yet as heavy as lead. I decide to see the doctor!

The doctor's visit. He is a jolly, big man, with black hair and pronounced jaw, whose fine eyes seem always to be witnessing the birth of some new and original thought. He is inspecting the sick and wounded in the porch of the church, distributing white powders, compounds of all colours, opium pills, painting chests with tincture of iodine, lancing blisters full of blood or pus. Two men carry up some poor being who writhes in their grasp, foaming at the corners of the mouth, and uttering savage cries: an epileptic in a fit!

I feel that above all things in heaven and earth I want to sleep. I obtain just as do the others some of the white compounds and a few morphia pills. At the same time I solicit permission to sleep in a barn, rather than in the open outside the village.

By chance I happened to encounter B—— that night. We spoke of comrades of pre-war days, canvassed events still recent, and yet how far off already! The meeting did me good, allaying the fever a little. A few hours' sleep and I woke up as fit as a lark and ready for anything, temporarily at least!

Friday, September 4th. Another day's march under a sun which seems to have increased in intensity even since yesterday. Jubécourt, Ville-sur-Cousances. These are full of *gendarmes* and *"forestiers"*; staff cars and supply lorries. All that spells retreat. . . . (*Censored.*) . . . Nevertheless, this has not the appearance of being a rout and I seek in vain to understand the meaning of these forced marches, of this breathless rush to Bar-le-Duc.

The most amazing and absurd rumours are flying round. Perhaps the pick of the bunch is the news that we are marching to Paris to maintain order!

Julvécourt, Ippécourt. We halt after leaving Fleury-sur-Aire, and here we eat. Batches of men arrive with huge portions of cheese which looks like Brie. Others are carrying bottles and cans fastened to their belts. The tins begin to rattle.

The grass in the meadow where we are resting is thick and wet. Many of the men take off their boots and walk barefooted to refresh their feet in the cool greenness. Almost all of us have spread our coats and tunics saturated with perspiration to dry in the sun. Clean shirts and the coloured linings of over-garments are everywhere. The colours dance in the bright sunshine, tiring the eyes.

In the cold and transparent waters of the Aire I wash myself to the waist. Two or three of the men have stripped themselves for a swim. Among them I notice a muscular, brown-skinned swimmer who disports himself vigorously, moving with a stroke which carries him from one side of the river to the other in a few seconds. All along the bank men are dabbling, bending over the water to wash socks and handkerchiefs. Little by little a blue film spreads over the surface and becomes iridescent in the sunshine. We dine gaily in the shade of some trees whose lower branches droop almost into the water. Near us a lieutenant with waxed moustache, arms bare, the open front of his shirt displaying a chest as hairy as that of a wild boar, is standing in the midst of a group of other men and holding forth. The loudness of his voice deafens and overcomes his listeners. At times, selections from his harangue reach me:

"There are two ways to settle them; break through the centre or outflank them on the wings."

Nubécourt. Today's march has not exhausted me as much as yesterday's. I venture to remind B——, the Maixenter, of a certain night I permitted him to pass in my bed. Poor me! The beast appeals to my good heart, to what he calls my knowledge of the world. He is weary, oh, so weary! and the bed is so narrow! Are there no others to be found in the village? Surely there are many others! I depart without any attempt to dissimulate my annoyance and disgust.

We mess in a kitchen similar to the others I have described— the yellow lights of candles casting weird shadows over everything. A thick-lipped cook serves us with a spoilt and unsatisfying concoction which leaves a flavour like ink in one's mouth.

Long and wearily I seek a bed. But all my efforts as well as those of a flat-figured but good-hearted girl, succeed in gaining me only one hour's sleep. And that hour I passed on some straw in a barn.

Saturday, September 5th.

Porchon laughingly tells me that the wine-merchant has disposed of the wine we ordered and at a much better price than we offered.

Beauzée-sur-Aire; Sommaisne. It is at this latter place that during a short halt I see the first of the *Bulletins des Armées,*

A family of ducks is swimming about in the Aisne, a mere stream passing through the centre of the village.

Rembercourt-aux-Pots. There is a beautiful church here of the sixteenth century, a trifle flat, maybe, and its lines rather spoilt by excessive richness of ornamentation. Trees line the road; each time we pass through the shade of them I carry my cap in my hand and experience an almost overwhelming desire to sit down and rest. More *gendarmes* and foresters, still more beflagged motorcars. This evidently is not the battle front! We pass a hamlet with a tiny station. That is the line doubtless on which tonight we will find ourselves en route to Paris (nothing else but Paris is talked about now).

Condé-en-Barrois. A long string of ammunition vans coming from the village blind us with an opaque dust. The midday halt takes place in a field in which everything is adance in the blinding heat. Some poor devil is brought before the captain. He is waisted with water-bottles and mess-tins from which peep forth bottles of wine and beer. In either hand he carries a pair of fowls flapping and croaking violently. Moreover, as he is holding a string of a package in his teeth, he finds it rather difficult to render an explanation. The package covers the lower part of his face; one can see only two distressed and tearful eyes. In due course he explains to us in a whining tone that he was arrested in the village at a moment when he was collecting provisions, but that he has paid for everything, that he is an honest man, that he would not for a second dream of stealing so much as a pin, that it is not fair to him. The words "looting" and "court-martial" descend upon his head with the stunning force of a mallet. He is commanded to take his provisions to the cook's quarters. And he departs ruefully, almost hidden beneath his collection of bottles, birds, packages and mess-tins.

I slept for two hours with P—— at the house of a bicycle merchant. The room was upside down, goods all piled up in one corner, yawning cupboards bare. Are the people doing this from motives of prudence, or have they received an order to evacuate?

It is the same in the house where we dine. The prevailing confusion is even more eloquent, for the house in question is more spacious and well built. Nothing in the sideboards; walls bare; the table itself seems lost in the cold solitude of the beeswaxed floor.

It is a feast we find in this village, which is larger than the others we have visited. Up to the present we have only passed through poor hamlets, cleaned out from top to bottom. The men make hay while the sun shines; mutton has been bought for them and they settle down to an orgy. It is long since they have touched wine. They have it now and they abuse it, also cider and beer.

Night has descended when we take up the march again. It is about ten o'clock. The column moves on its sinuous way with many alarms and unexpected halts. I hear behind me the steps of a horse in the saddle of which the captain of the 8th sleeps fitfully. He rouses himself from time to time to give a piece of his mind to certain men whose copious libations of the afternoon now impel to stop abruptly and frequently. One of these men replies to him impertinently, protesting that it is inhuman to drive men onwards in the way he is doing, and then discreetly vanishes into the ranks before he can be identified.

We are returning the way we came, and we do not stop at the tiny station in the village I had noticed earlier in the day. Are we not then going to entrain at Bar-le-Duc? Do they then intend to let the disorder at Paris continue?

Here we are at Rembercourt, silently marching past darkened houses. We pass the road to Sommaisne on the left and cut across fields towards some woods vaguely outlined against the sky.

4

The Days of the Marne

Sunday, September 6th,

Half-past one in the morning! Kit bags on the ground, rifles piled, lines in sections of four, at the edge of a little wood of birch trees struggling for life on a stony soil. The night is cold. I place a listening post well forward and return and seat myself near my men. The stillness is palpitating; the passage of time interminably long-drawn. The dawn begins to lighten the sky. I look around me and see the pale and tired faces of my men.

Four o'clock. A dozen rifle shots to the right cause me to leap to my feet just as I am making myself comfortable. Out of a small neighbouring wood a dozen *Uhlans* are flying at a gallop—they must have passed the night in the covert.

The day breaks clear and fresh. My Nubécourt bedfellow produces his inexhaustible flask, and we sip a drop of brandy which possesses no bouquet at all and seems like raw alcohol. The captain joins us at last and explains the situation in a few words:

"A German army corps," he says, "is marching towards the south-east, having for flank-guard a brigade which follows the valley of the Aire. The ——th Corps is going to engage the said German corps, while it remains for us to deal with the flanking brigade."

For the first time I am going to experience war in all its reality!

Facing the Aire, with Sommaisne behind us, the men commence to dig trenches with their handy entrenching tools. They know it is intended that we should fight, and they need no urging to put forth their best efforts. Before us and to the left towards Pretz-en-Argonne a battalion covers us. Through my glasses I see two watchful observers on the roof of a house.

The trenches are finished. They are only deep enough to shelter us kneeling, but that is sufficient.

Towards nine o'clock the bombardment commences. High explosives hurtle by without pause, bursting over Pretz, shattering roofs and bringing down whole walls. My men remain quite calm although they know that a violent and furious fight is immediately before them.

Eleven o'clock and our turn is come. The men deploy instantly. There is no time for reflection on my part; I feel nothing, unless it be that the fevered fatigue of the past hours has now left me. Rifles are speaking close at hand, shells are still bursting in the distance. With a strange detachment I watch the lines of our men blue and red against the earth, advancing and advancing apparently without movement. About me the wheat bows down beneath a heavy, languid breeze, and with a certain feverishness I repeat to myself again and again: "I am in it now! This is war and I am in it!" and I am astonished to see that all the things about me retain their ordinary appearance, to hear the snapping of rifles which is no more than the snapping of rifles. For, on the other hand, it almost seems as if my body had undergone some change, that it is no longer the same, that I experience different sensations with different organs.

"Lie down!"

The bullets are whistling above us now. The rattle of the fusillade drowns their sharp notes; but I know that behind us the song of the bullets dies away to diminuendo and silence.

We commence to advance. The movement is admirably executed, with the same regularity and deliberation as if we were at manoeuvres. Little by little there arises in me an exhilaration which raises me above myself. I feel that all these men are part of myself—these men who, at a gesture from me push forward despite the bullets shrilling towards us seeking chests, faces; the living flesh for billets.

We lie down for cover, we rise with a jump; we run as fast as our legs will carry us straight for the hidden Boches—we long to see those Boches so that we can get at them more surely and chase them far from these fields ruined and trampled by their hordes.

We are completely exposed and under fire. The bullets sing no longer; they pass invisible with a nasty spiteful hiss. They are no longer at play but in deadly earnest.

Clac! Clac! Two bullets have struck immediately to my left. The noise at once surprises and slightly amazes me; these bullets seem less dangerous when they sing and whistle. Clac! Clac! Stones, pieces of dried earth, spurts of dust fly into the air; we have been seen and they have got the range of us. Forward! I am leading, seeking a ditch, a slope, a fold in the earth wherein to shelter my men after the first rush—even the hedge of a field, or anything which will render them less visible to the Boches will do. A movement of my right arm shortens the line by half. I hear the tramp of feet, the rustle of the stubble lying in our course. And while we are running forward the detachment in support fires rapidly but steadily. Then when I raise my cap, that detachment in its turn charges at the double, whilst all around me my men's rifles come into play and speak unceasingly.

A strangled cry to the left. I have scarcely time to see the man sprawl flat on his back, his two legs still moving as though to carry him forward. A second, and all his body stiffens and then relaxes and the man is no more than an inert thing, dead flesh which tomorrow the sun will commence to decompose.

Forward! To remain still would cost us more dearly now than the most furious assault. Forward! The men are falling rapidly, stopped dead in full course, some crashing prone without a word, others halting and staring stupidly, while feeling with their hand for their wound. And they say: "I have got it," or, "Mine has arrived!" Often it is no more than a single expressive word. Almost all of them, even those whose wounds are slight, turn pale at the shock. The impression is borne in upon me that one thought alone is in all their minds; to get away very quickly, never mind where, so long as it be somewhere free from this eternal hissing of the bullets. They seem to me like little children, children whom one would wish to console, to protect. An almost insane desire seizes me to cry out to those waiting ahead of us:

"Do not harm them! You have no right to do so! They are no longer soldiers—they will do you no harm!"

Instead I say to one of the passing men:

"Come along, old man, cheer up! Thirty yards ahead of you, behind that little crest, you will be out of danger . . . ah, yes, I know your foot is bad, that it swells. But we will take good care of you in a minute. Do not be afraid."

The man, a corporal, dragging himself along on all fours, stops to look back at me with the eyes of a caged beast. Then he resumes his clumsy, tormented, crablike crawl.

At last I catch a glimpse of the Boches. They are hiding themselves behind sheaves which they push before them; but at least I know now where they are and my men's bullets will therefore stand a better chance of finding an objective.

The advance is resumed and continues without wavering. A great confidence possesses me. I feel that all is going well;—and at this moment a corporal arrives breathless and covered with perspiration:

"Lieutenant."

"What is it? "

"The Major sends me to tell you you are too far advanced. The movement has been executed too quickly. You must halt and await orders."

I lead my section to the shelter of a slight undulation which is no more than a vaguely-defined fold in the earth, but where at least some shelter from the bullets will be obtained. And so we remain there lying flat, awaiting the orders which appear as if they will never arrive. Everywhere, above us, before us, to the right and the left, the shots whistle and hiss and shrill. A few steps from me the bullets of a deafening machine-gun strike the earth in a regular, steady stream. Dust and stones are flung high in the air, and for a moment I feel an almost irresistible temptation to approach that death-dealing squall, and touch that invisible stream of innumerable and minute splinters of metal, each of which can kill.

The minutes drag past long and wearying. I raise myself a little and attempt to see what is occurring. To the left the thin line of riflemen extend as far as eye can reach; all the men are lying behind their knapsacks firing. Behind a wheatfield, twenty men or so are standing to aim better and fire. I can see distinctly the recoil of their rifles and the corresponding jerk of their right shoulders. As the smoke clears for a second, I am able to distinguish Porchon's platoon, and Porchon himself smoking a cigarette. There also is the Saint Maixenter's platoon, somewhat disorganized. Further away again are the men of the 8th. Behind them a little man is walking up and down, erect, nonchalant and quite at home. Who can this reckless individual be? Through my glasses I make out an over-waxed moustache and the blue smoke of a pipe; it is the captain! Someone had already told me of his attitude when under fire!

The orders, merciful Heavens, where are our orders? What can be the matter? Why are they leaving us here? I make up my mind and suddenly get up. It is imperative I should know what the Boches are doing and where they are at present. Keeping under cover of the sheaves, I mount the gentle slope until I reach the top of it. There before me, four or five hundred yards distant, are men in greyish green uniforms, almost indistinguishable from the greenness of the fields. It is only with the greatest difficulty I can make them out at all.

Quite near their line, but far to my right, is a machine-gun surrounded by men in French uniform firing at triple speed. I determine to bring my men to the top of the slope where at least they will be able to fire.

While I am making my way back to them a shell passes overhead. It explodes among the detachment of the 8th, and a gap of twenty yards is made in their line. The next second other men have filled the gap. A second explosion, another and still another; the bombardment has recommenced. All my men fling themselves flat.

"Oh! . . ." The cry escaped a dozen of us at once. A high explosive burst clean among the Saint Maixenter's platoon. And he, I saw it distinctly with my own eyes, received the shell full in his body. His cap vanished into space, a part of his coat, an arm. And there he is lying on the earth a shapeless mass, white and red pulp, a body stripped wellnigh naked, shattered. His men, finding themselves leaderless, give way and scatter.

What is this? . . . Can it be that the confusion is spreading to all the men on the left there? It travels rapidly towards us. Some soldiers are running towards Sommaisne beneath the shells. When each shell explodes it makes a gap among them, blowing away men as you blow away dust with a puff. The confusion has spread to the 8th now. If the captain were only there, he would be able to hold his men. But a few moments ago I saw him press a hand swiftly to his face. Our covering section away to the left comes next; the bullets have left none to preserve discipline. Now it is the neighbouring platoon. Then suddenly, brutally, we are swept up by the wave: there are the unknown faces of men of other companies round about us mixing with the men and destroying their nerve. A tall thin man, the captain of the 5th, cries out to me that the commander has ordered us to fight in retreat, that we haven't been supported in time, that we are alone and lost if we remain. And thus is the position abandoned.

With all my power I strive to preserve order and calm, to allay the panic among my men. I march deliberately with arms wide extended, exclaiming:

"Do not run, do not run! Follow me." All my attention is concentrated on the task of getting my men away to safety with as little loss as possible. One of them near me receives a bullet through his skull while engaged in cutting an opening through some wire; he falls on to the wire and remains hanging there, broken in two, his feet touching the earth on the one side, head and arms hanging down over the other.

Shells follow us, high explosive and shrapnel. Three times I find myself within the deadly cone of bursting shrapnel: the bullets hiss into the earth about me, smashing heads and shattering feet.

We march through an inferno of smoke, from time to time obtaining a glimpse, through momentary clearings, of the village and the river running beneath the trees. But there is no truce to the shells which follow us in hundreds.

I recollect passing one of my sergeants being carried by two of the men on crossed rifles; he pointed out to me speechlessly, his torn and bloodstained shirt and his side terribly lacerated by an explosion. I could see the raw edges of the flesh. . . .

I march onwards and onwards exhausted and stumbling. I take a long gulp of the water that remains in my flask. Since yesterday evening I have eaten nothing.

When we reach the edge of the stream, the men halt and throw themselves down and commence to lap the muddied waters like dogs.

It must be seven o'clock now; the sun is sinking into a bed of virgin gold. The sky above us is a pale and transparent emerald. The earth darkens, colours vanish. It is quite dark by the time we leave Sommaisne. We become mere shadows trailing along the road.

We halt for the first time at Rembercourt. Nothing but sleep seems to matter now, and I fling myself down on the bare earth, calling upon it. Before it descends upon me I hear the rolling over all the roads of the wagons and ambulance vans filled with the wounded; and further away, back in Sommaisne, the smashing of rifle butts against closed doors and the harsh savage cries of the looting Teutons.

Monday, September 7th.

The morning mist awakens me. My clothes are drenched and drops of water glisten on the mica of my map case. Before us and a little to the left is Rembercourt, whose large church dominates the village in its shadow. From where we are, we can see one side of it in all its length. Towards the left there is a little road which disappears between two slopes.

It is along that road that the captain and Porchon appear towards ten o'clock accompanied by a handful of men. It appears that they found themselves cut off from the rest of the regiment and passed the night in a wood in advance of the French line. I was able to identify the Captain while he was still some distance off by means of a lance which he carried; it was an *Uhlan's* lance, captured at Gibercy, and with which nothing could induce him to part. I made my report to him.

As at Cuisy, we dig trenches. Are we going to wait here for the Germans this time? We no longer have the advantage of a valley before us as at Dannevoux, but in the course of the five hundred yards or so which intervene between our new position and Rembercourt, I estimate that should the Germans elect to advance along this road many of them will fall before they reach us.

Towards Beauzée the fight is still in progress. Unendingly little groups of wounded men appear over the last crest and march slowly towards us. Those with arms in slings move more quickly; others drag along, helping themselves with sticks cut in some small wood or other; many halt, then drag themselves a few yards further, then pause again.

During the afternoon I went down into the village. It was full of soldiers ... (*Censored*) ...

(*Censored.*)

Soon after three o'clock the German heavy artillery commences to shell Rembercourt. At five o'clock the church takes fire. The crimson glow of the conflagration is emphasized as the shadows increase. The blackness of the night makes the church an immense brazier. The wooden framework of the roof is traced out in flames and incandescence. The steeple has become a living fire in the heart of which the dead bells hang black and grim.

The framework of the roof falls piecemeal. One can see the rafters sagging and sagging and then remaining suspended for a few moments above the furnace before falling with a deafening crash. And each time a portion falls in this way, a volcano of clear sparks rises high into the sky to remain drifting and floating like some echo.

For hours and hours I stood watching the fire, my heart sad and heavy. My men are asleep on the ground, lining the trench with their bodies. Try as I will I cannot lie down to sleep like them.

Tuesday, September 8th,

The captain roused me I don't know how many times to give me instructions; as a matter of fact I believe it was because he himself found sleep impossible and was lonely with that loneliness which visits men on such nights. Together with his liaison officers he had taken up sleeping quarters in a dense thicket by the roadside. At each

49

awakening I beheld the church still in flames.

This morning the ruins were still smoking. The mass of fire-blackened stone stood clearly defined against a limpid sky.

The men are sleeping heavily... (*Censored.*) ...

(*Censored.*)

From some woods away to the left a fusillade growing more and more violent each instant rings out. Behind us a battery of 120 mm.'s speak without pausing. And above Rembercourt at long intervals shells burst, half a dozen at a time.

(*Censored.*)

..., lying on a slope when the shriek of the shells announce the arrival of the Germans, then, quite placidly resume their task again.

(*Censored.*)

This morning someone offered me some brandy plums, huge greengages preserved in a narrow bottle, cherries in a thick syrup, green haricots and peas in bottles, as well as some pink sweetmeats arranged artistically beneath laced paper in a pale blue box on the cover of which, inscribed in letters of gold, was the name "Pamphile."

(*Censored.*)

At noon we leave the trenches. Marching in loose columns we move towards the road which runs from Rembercourt to Vauxmarie. All along the road from Erize-la-Petite we encounter the craters the shells have dug in the fields. The countryside is bare and depressing, despite the brilliant sunshine. In a ditch lie some horses, disembowelled, legs shattered, huddled at the bottom of the sloping sides. There were six of them all in a heap, making an enormous pile of carrion, the horrible stagnant smell of which saturated the air. Everywhere there are shattered ammunition carts, wheels in splinters, ironwork twisted.

Vauxmarie Road. We take up a position, availing ourselves of the ditch as a trench, ready to support those fighting ahead. There is a great desolate plain before us, ploughed by shells, sown with still bodies and fragments of the uniforms of men with faces turned either towards the sky or buried in the earth, rifles lying beside them just as they had fallen from their hands. To the right the road mounts towards the top of the valley; it is of a dazzling whiteness that tires the eyes. Far before us a number of platoons are lying on the ground in extended order, only to be distinguished with difficulty. They are receiving the full force of the German artillery.

Abruptly the shells cease ravaging the uncultivated and shattered fields and come towards us. They arrive shrieking and all together. Nearer and nearer they come, until we are certain they are going to descend upon us. And the men hunch their bodies together, round their backs, thrust their heads beneath their knapsacks, all their muscles contracting in agonized suspense while waiting the explosion of those enormous messengers of death. The bombardment increases in intensity, and now plumes of black smoke are drifting along the hilltop and the noise becomes ear-splitting. Each time a shell falls in the ranks there ensues, in the real sense of the term, a scattering of the men; and when the smoke has dispersed there remain lying on the yellow earth of the stubble field dark sombre patches, forms vague and unmoving.

A commander of the *gendarmerie* mounts the hillside on his bicycle, pedalling with all his strength. He is making directly for the point where the line of the valley touches the sky crowned with its sinister black plumes. Smaller and smaller he becomes, is silhouetted for a moment clear and distinct, and finally vanishes. A quarter of an hour passes before he reappears, a streak, now pedalling back into the valley. He has a message for our commander; it seems that something is required of us.

We are conducted back to the heights of Rembercourt, passing to the right of the village. Here we take cover on a steep slope covered with wild vegetation, extending alongside the orchard which I had seen that morning. The bursting shells almost deafen us. They explode in hundreds, shattering the plain, obliterating the road along which we marched a short time since, causing tiles to fall and rattling the woodwork of roofs. Nor are we forgotten. A few compliments in the form of half a dozen high explosives are generously sent our way. The last of these burst so close to our commander, who was sitting on the slope, that it seemed as if someone had punched him violently and rudely in the back. Under the tremendous force of the explosions the trees of the orchard bend and sway, causing a shower of plums and apples to fall upon us.

We have not been sighted, but the enemy knows the lie of the land so well that he guesses without difficulty the probable location of our reserves, and punishes them by way of precaution. Up to the present, however, all my men have escaped without serious injury, except one who, descending the slope, suddenly mounted into the air to come to the earth behind us. At least ten men received scratches.

Happily we leave before the enemy devotes serious attention to us. At a certain moment, immediately following the arrival of a shell, a messenger rushed out of the village where the captain had taken up his station. He came running towards us, gesticulating violently. While he was still several yards away he cried in a loud voice:

"Advance!"

Raising my sword I repeat the order.

"Forward! Follow me!"

And I jump down on to the road. Hardly have I taken three steps forward, however, before I hear the shells come shrieking towards us. There is just time for the men to rush back up the slope they had already quitted; in the very act of throwing myself flat the shells explode six at once. A portion of the road rises towards Heaven to descend again in a hail of stones and earth.

The smell almost suffocates me as I lie clinging to the earth there, shrouded in dense black smoke. I think that was a narrow escape! A few moments of calm succeed. Now is the time to run: the men come down the slope at their best speed; then, finding ourselves outside the zone of immediate danger and sheltered a little by the village, we mount a rising behind which I know we may hope to find a certain amount of safety.

More shells fall on the spot we occupied a few moments since. My men look at each other, look at me, and congratulate themselves. The narrowness of their escape loosens their tongues. "Ah, the filthy dogs!" I hear. That also is what the messenger calls them when I see him again. On the road he had not sufficient breath left to express his feelings. He had been so near the explosion area that the buckles of his knapsack were shattered, and when afterwards he looked around it was to find himself occupying a post of honour in the middle of a field, innocent of a scratch, while the said knapsack hung gracefully among the branches of a plumtree.

The day declines; we go back once more to our trenches. I met, sitting in a ditch, two cavalry subalterns, one a Hussar, the other a *Chasseur*, belonging to some detachment or other. I had made their acquaintance at the depot.

(*Censored.*)

Night has fallen and once again we have forgotten to eat. A mouthful of iron rations, a drop of tepid water from lay flask, which water has a pronounced taste of tin.—"*Still, that is something else the Prussians won't have,"* as my grandmother used to say.

Wednesday, September 9th.

Not a wink of sleep. The noise of the shells hurtling through the air is constantly in my ears, while the acrid and suffocating fumes of explosives haunt my nostrils. Scarcely yet is it midnight before I receive orders to depart. I emerge from the trusses of wheat and rye among which I had ensconced myself. Bits of stalk have slipped down my collar and up my sleeves, and tickle me all over. The night is so dark that we stumble over the stones and irregularities of the ground. We pass very close to some 120's drawn up behind us; I hear the voices of the artillerymen, but only with difficulty can I distinguish the heavy, sleeping guns.

Rations are distributed *en route* with no other light than that of a camp lantern which gives forth but a faint glow. The feeble yellow light stains with brown patches the portions of raw meat cut up in the dusty grass of the roadside.

A march across fields, a march of somnambulists, mechanical, legs light as down, heads heavy as lead. It seems to last for hours and hours. And we are always bearing to the left; at daybreak, I assure myself, we shall have returned to our point of departure. Little by little the shadows rise, enabling me to recognize the Vauxmarie Road, the wrecked ammunition carts, the dead horses.

Hallo! The German guns are speaking early this morning! Before us shrapnel is bursting noisily and spitefully. Over the plain they have thrown a barrage. Nevertheless we have to go through it. Our first section detaches itself; in a line, long-drawn and thin, it moves across the fields towards a small wood which the captain has indicated as the objective. Rifles crackle away to the left. Bullets sing and throw up the dust about the marching section. Then shrapnel bursts right over the men. The undulating line becomes still, taking cover behind a ridge of earth shaped like a gigantic caterpillar, I have been given to understand that we are to occupy the advance post, and I await my turn to move forward. The major and the captain are before us, taking cover of some trees, watching. And the captain, seeing his men out there under the shower of shells, finds it difficult to make up his mind to throw us others forward. After a time the commander of the gendarmerie whom I had seen cycling along the road, comes up. He is crimson to the lips and his eyes are savagely glaring. Cursing and swearing violently, he utters a few breathless words.

(*Censored.*)

The captain, turning towards me, said: "Go!"

So the time is come!

I experience a feeling only of pleasure. I am in the same strange mental condition as when under fire for the first time at Sommaisne. My legs move without volition; I march unthinkingly, conscious only of an all-pervading joy which elevates me above myself and permits me as it were to look upon myself as another being. In five minutes we reach the pine-wood which is our destination. We deploy before it, indeed almost within it. Without waiting a minute, the men set to work with their trenching tools. At the end of a couple of hours we possess a deep and narrow trench. Behind us to the left is Rembercourt; to the right front the tiny station of Vauxmarie.

The heat is enervating and unhealthy. A few clouds drift slowly past, increasing in size little by little and growing darker and more ominous, while the edges yet remain fringed with silver. From time to time puffs of wind bring to us a stench, sickly, penetrating, intolerable. It is as though we were in a charnel house.

All around us are bodies. One there is that is most horrible to look upon. Yet look upon it I must, despite my will. It is the body of a man lying near a shell hole; the head is detached from the trunk, and the blackened entrails protrude from a terrible wound in the abdomen. Near him lies a sergeant, the stock of his rifle still in his hands—the barrel and mechanism must have been blown far away. Another man lies with both legs parallel, yet the foot of one crosses the other; that leg must be shattered. And there are so many others! Our position compels us to look upon them, to breathe that foetid air until nightfall.

And until nightfall I smoke and smoke in an attempt to stifle the soul-sickening miasma, that smell of the poor dead, lost on the field of battle, abandoned by their own who had not the time to throw even a few lumps of earth over them to hide them from the eyes of the living.

Throughout the day aeroplanes hovered over us. Shells fell also. But our captain had had a keen eye for a good place, and while a few explosions came perilously near, we suffered no casualties. At the worst it was a few shrapnel or other shells which burst far too high overhead to cause us concern.

For what reason are the aeroplanes remaining so long aloft up there? For more than two hours they have floated above us, describing great circles, drawing away only when our artillery became too pressing in its attentions, then returning until the black crosses on their wings were easily and plainly discernible. Towards evening they headed directly for the heavy black clouds accumulating on the horizon.

Into those sombre masses the sun sinks, dyeing them crimson at first, leaden as the light slowly fades. The finish of the day is ominous and depressing. The darkness of night settles down almost tangibly, while the stench of the dead bodies rises and spreads.

Sitting at the bottom of the trench, my hands crossed over my raised knees, I hear before and behind me, over the whole plain, the sharp thud of pickaxes against stones, the scraping of spades throwing up the earth, the careful murmur of lowered voices. Occasionally, some man whom one cannot see, coughs and expectorates. The night envelops and hides us from the enemy's eyes, permitting us at last to bury our dead.

The voice of my sergeant calls to me through the darkness:

"Are you there. Lieutenant?"

"Yes, I am here!"

Groping about until he finds my hand, he places something into it.

"Here, sir. This is all we found on them."

Crouching at the bottom of the trench, I strike a match. In the light it sheds for a brief spell, I see a much-worn pocket book, a leather purse, and an identification disc attached to a piece of black cord. A second match! The pocket book contains the photograph of a young woman nursing a baby in her lap; also I am enabled to make out a name inscribed in straggling letters on the disc. The sergeant comments:

"There was nothing on the other—I searched him from his heels to his—his neck—I mean the one whose head was blown off. And there was nothing except the purse which belonged to him."

A third match. The purse contains a little money, a few coppers only, and a piece of dirty, crumpled paper, on which is written: "Gronin Charles, Railway employee. Class, 1904. Soissons." Then the match goes out.

I shake the sergeant's hand; it is damp and feverish, and the fingers are not steady.

"Goodnight! Go and sleep! Go on!"

He departs, leaving me solitary and alone in the midst of fast sleeping men. To sleep like them! . . . To be able to stifle all thought, to forget! In my hand the little possessions of the dead men grow heavier and heavier. . . . "Gronin Charles, railway employee. . . ."The smiling faces of the photograph dance beneath my closed eyelids, grow bigger and bigger until they become almost a hallucination. The poor, poor people!

Thursday, September 10th.

Something plashes gently on my face: raindrops large and tepid. Have I indeed been asleep, then? And what time can it be? The wind is rising, but the night is still black. A little to the right front of the trench a dark mass is outlined against the still darker sky. That must be the heaped-up bundles of straw in which the major, the captain and his messengers have ensconced themselves for the night.

I have just settled to sleep again when a few bullets whistle over-head. It seems to me that they come from close at hand. Yet we, being the advance posts, can have no other detachments before us. What does it mean then?

I am not permitted much time for speculation; abruptly, a con-centrated fusillade breaks out, every second approaching nearer and nearer and extending the whole length of the line. Without doubt, those are Germans firing, directing a night attack against us.

"On your feet, every man of you. On your feet. Quick. Get up!"

I shake a corporal sleeping near me. From one end of the line to the other a shiver passes, followed by the quick rustling of straw; then bayonets clatter, and magazines click.

All this has passed in an instant, yet I have still had time to see the major and the captain jump back down into the trench away to the right, and scarcely have they done so before black figures are silhou-etted, barely discernible against the lightless sky, over the top of the nearest rising. They were not thirty yards away when I distinguished the pointed spikes of their helmets. That sight was more than suffi-cient. At the top of my lungs I issue an order for rapid fire.

Hardly has the command left my lips when the dense masses of men rapidly approaching us burst into shrill, savage shouts.

"Hurrah! Hurrah! *Vorwärts!* "How many thousands of soldiers are surging down upon us then? The moist earth quivers beneath the tramp of their heavy feet. Most surely must we be smashed to pieces, trampled down, broken. For there are not more than sixty of us all told, and how may sixty men extended in single file hope to resist the tremendous pressure of these ranks upon ranks of men rushing down upon us like a herd of maddened buffaloes?

"Rapid fire! *Nom de Dieu!* Fire!" The crackling of the rifles rends the air; spurts of flame shatter the darkness. The rifles of my platoon have spoken simultaneously!

And now there is a gap in the very heart of the charging mass. I hear shrill screams of agony as of beasts mortally stricken. The dark figures divide to flow right and left, just as if, before the trench, and extending its whole length, a tempest had raged and laid men to the earth, as the breath of the gale bends down the growing wheat.

Some of the men about me say:

"Look, Lieutenant! See, they are lying down!"

"No, my friend! It is not so. They have fallen down!"

And . . . (*Censored.*)

Once more I repeat:

"Fire! Fire! Let them have it! Put it into them! Fire!"

The men reload their magazines swiftly, resting their cheeks . . . (*Censored.*) . . . and fire a volley at point blank range. Out there, men fall in swathes! The gap widens and widens until no one remains standing before us, not a living soul! But the shadows nevertheless are still moving onwards to the right and left; they intend to outflank, to envelop us. And to the right and left there is not a man to stem for a moment that rushing torrent, which, at the best, we have only been able to check for an instant, and divert to either side. The wave will reform behind us—all will be lost!

"Hurrah! *Vorwärts!*"

They excite themselves with their own cries, like savages. Their raucous voices rise loud above the crackling rifle fire, toned and modulated in the flux of the wind-driven rain and the louder detonations close at hand. Suddenly the wind has increased; the rain descends literally in torrents: one gains the impression that the fury of the fighters has moved the very heavens.

All at once a flame leaps up, glistening on brass buckles and helmet spikes, turning bayonets to silver. The Germans have set fire to the pile of straw beneath which the major and captain were snugly sleeping a short while since. The flames writhe and waver this way and that at the wind's caprice; drops of rain flying before the glow become like the spray of a rushing fountain. The faces of my men are pale and streaming with water; their eyes, under frowning brows, are dark-ringed and like sparks of steel, expressing at once their eagerness to strike and kill as well as to live.

"First section, right face! . . ."

Can they hear me? . . .

"Right face! . . ."

They do not hear me. The unceasing spatter of rifle fire, the moaning wind, the rain beating a tattoo on mess tins, and above all, the shouting of human voices drown my command.

"Let me pass, you!"

I thrust a man against the parapet of the trench.

"Let me pass!"

From man to man I progress, calling aloud for the sergeant. One, two, three soldiers I pass, and then before me the trench is empty, abandoned; a little trampled straw, a rifle, a few knapsacks and nothing more. But I am just in time to catch one dark figure of a man hauling himself out of the trench by the over-hanging brambles.

"Hey, you!" I cry. "The major? The captain? . . ."

The wind hurls a few disconnected words into my face.

"Have left . . . orders!"

At that moment two helmeted figures appear above the parapet someway further along to the right, two figures silhouetted against the light of the fire. The next instant something falls heavily on to the straw at the bottom of the trench.

Meanwhile behind me the shrieking Germans are right on the top of my men. Obviously there is nothing to do but try and win through to the trenches of a battalion of *chasseurs* located to the rear and right of our line.

I give the order with all the strength of my lungs.

"Pass through the wood! Not alongside it! Retreat into the wood!"

I thrust forward the men who instinctively hesitate before the dense entanglement of branches bristling with thorns, and I in my turn bodily fling myself into the undergrowth. To the left of my trench ring out oaths and strangled cries. Apparently, some fools afraid of the thorns have hesitated too long and now perhaps have German bayonets in back or chest!

I start to run towards the *chasseurs'* line. Before me and all around me dark shadows move; and always the same cry rings out:

"Hurrah! *Vorwärts!*"

I am surrounded by Boches; it seems impossible that I can escape, separated as I am from all my men. Nevertheless I grasp my revolver in my hand and pray only I may be permitted to give a good account of myself.

Suddenly I am sprawling face downwards, nose to the earth, having stumbled over something hard and metallic. Lying in the mud is the body of a dead German whose helmet has rolled a little away from him. Instantly an idea seizes me. I pick up the helmet and place it on my own head, passing the strap beneath my chin to secure it.

There follows a mad flight for the safety the *chasseurs* will afford. Without hesitating a second, I rush by groups of Boches who are wandering about doubtfully, their original plans having been rather upset by our fusillade. As I pass them I cry:

"Hurrah! *Vorwärts!*"

Like them, too, I keep repeating the word to which they seem to attach great importance, which is:

"*Heiligtum!*"

The rain stings my face: the mud adheres to my soles until only with difficulty can I raise boots which have become enormously big and heavy. Twice I fall on my hands and knees, only to rise again and instantly resume my flight, notwithstanding my aching legs. Singing and whistling bullets pass over me into the darkness beyond.

Out of the blackness at my feet a man rises and the words on his lips are French.

"Is it you, Letty?"

"Yes, Lieutenant; I've got one in the thigh."

"That's all right, old man; we'll get there yet!"

Already there are no more harsh voiced brawlers around us. Manifestly they must reform before continuing the assault. So I throw away the helmet and replace my cap of which I have taken good care.

Before reaching the *chasseurs* I overtake four Boches, in each of whom, either in the back or in the head, I put a revolver bullet. Each one drops in his tracks with a long, strangled cry.

(*Censored.*)

In the *chasseurs'* trenches I discover twenty or so of my men. They are kneeling in the mud at the bottom, unable to find a place in the firing line.

"Follow me, my boys," I cried.

The Vauxmarie Road is only a few steps away and I place my twenty *poilus* along the sloping side of a ditch. One and all we feel that all we want to do is to remain there until we die.

Still another outburst of rifles. Flat on my stomach on the water-sodden grass I look upon a second fire the reflection of whose ruddy glow seems to be carved out of the night's opacity—that must be the Vauxmarie farm burning.

Behind us a voice unexpectedly rings out:

"*Ohé!* Trenches there? Is there anyone of the ——th here."

I reply: "Present."

"An officer?"

"I am Lieutenant. Who is asking?"

"It is I, Lieutenant."

A man presents himself to me and tells me he has been sent by Captain C——.

"Come quickly . . . quickly, with every man you can find. The flag is near here among the trees and the captain is afraid that unless he has assistance he will not be able to save it."

We set out instantly following the orderly.

Our trousers cling to our knees and thighs; the long grass pours water into our boots.

We pass a machine-gun section. The men have attached the belt; but they have only one gun and that won't work.

Hoarse cries rise again, increased to the point of frenzy, then weaken and finally die away. The *chasseurs* are holding fast! One of my men exclaim:

"And *that's* their stopping place."

Easily I follow the sounds of the fight. All my senses appear to have become abnormally sharp. And so I am able to perceive some vaguely defined dark figures who move silently not twenty yards away to the right of us. I strive with all my force to pierce the darkness, but my eyes are filled with water and fail me. So, motioning with my hand, I say in a low voice to one of my men:

"Look there, Chabeau. Can you see anything?"

"Yes, Lieutenant."

"What is it?"

"Some Boches. They are flanking us."

"Are there many of them?"

"No, not a pile of them."

"Can you count them?"

Two or three seconds and then:

"I believe there are seven of them."

His words confirm my own conclusions. A few stragglers, undoubtedly, who have lost their way in this infernal mêlée of the night.

At my order ten of my men face towards the right, and in each one's ear I whisper:

"Wait until I give the word to fire. Do not hurry and aim well."

The Boches have halted, hesitating, undecided; they form a dark group framed in a stillness which seems almost palpitating.

"Fire!"

A spurt of flame, followed instantly by cries of agony and terror: "*Kamerad! Kamerad!*"

Only two remain standing and they rush towards me. The younger of them snatches at my hands covering them with tears and saliva. He utters a few incoherent words which reveal the tempest of fear obsessing him:

"I am not a Prussian; I am a Swabian. The Swabians have never done you any harm . . . the Swabians did not want this war. . . ."

And his eyes glare into mine in a very frenzy of revolting supplication.

"I have given the French wounded, water. My comrades also: that is what we Swabians are!"

He talks and talks, and always the same monotonous refrain is repeated:

"*Das machen die Schzuaben,* That is what the Swabians do."

Then, with ever mounting incoherence, he tells me other things; that he is an electrician, that he can walk fifty yards on his hands . . . he would have done it instantly too if I had but given the signal, possessed as he was by terrible fear, tortured by the thirst for life.

The other was passed from one man to another, palpitating and terror-stricken: we had not so far made any other prisoners! My men jeered at him like curious children. They listened with an air of wisdom to the conversation between myself and the German. Not ill-naturedly they amused themselves by causing him involuntarily to hunch his neck down between his shoulders when they placed a hand upon him. And each time, they laughed heartily and boyishly.

All this time the crackling of rifles disturbs the night's stillness; the short snappy reports emanating close at hand, the swift whistling of German bullets from the distance. Nor did the rain cease to fall, plastering our great-coats on to our backs, streaming in rivulets from the peaks of our caps. The wind, however, had ceased to moan. It blew gently now as though appeased, but cold and foxy. The day was approaching and never was the light of day so longed for. I saw once more the battlefield of Sommaisne, bathed in sunlight, clear in outline, rich in colour. And all that night we had been as blind men, fighting gropingly. I shrank from the thought of death in that icy mud, or in those puddles of water into which one stumbled. . . .

How strange everything is. During a brief calm, music, strange, sharp, but rhythmic rings out. That must be the German bugles taking up their message and approaching nearer and nearer all along their lines. I turned to my Boche and asked:

"What is that?"

He bends his head, places his hand behind his ear to listen and replies:

"Halt!"

Truly enough the firing begins to die away little by little. A few more violent outbursts succeed, and then there is silence, except for stray shots here and there, which echo with curious loudness in the motionless, cold air. The stillness that follows seems almost menacing. It falls over the scene of battle like an immense mantle—it is a portentous silence, as though willed by some mysterious powers of evil: pregnant has the night been with human anguish and suffering.

The advent of the wan day does not lighten our spirits; a faint luminance, whitened and cloud-flecked, appears above the horizon, moving slowly towards the zenith. Storm battalions move languidly across the pale sky. The day is false to its season, presaging as it does, and so long in advance, the coming of winter. It is like one of those cold days which invariably arrive inopportunely to shatter the illusion of spring, just when one has commenced to delight in the new year's rush of life.

Not for a moment does the rain cease; steadily and stubbornly it falls now, swamping us and penetrating our clothing. One of the Germans remarks to me in a tone of familiarity:

"I am freezing!"

With hands in his pockets, elbows pressed close to his sides and shoulders hunched up, he is shivering while lounging at ease.

The minutes drag slowly by. At daybreak the colonel appears, his cavalry cloak stiff and heavy with mud. About a dozen prisoners are brought before him. I bring mine up also. The electrician will not leave my side, but clings to me desperately in a renewed access of terror, haunted probably by a vision of himself back to a wall facing a dozen levelled rifles, ready at word of command to place a dozen bullets through him.

There is a junior officer among the prisoners whose lips and chin are hidden by a curly beard. He understands a few words of French, and, as the colonel questions him, he stares directly back at him through slitted eyes and answers:

"Yes, *monsieur.*"

"Not *monsieur*, but Colonel!"

The words, uttered in a sharp voice, are accompanied by a meaning glance. The Boche flinches as though he had received a cut from a stirrup leather. He draws himself up, arms to the body, shoulders squared, stiffly at attention.

Captain C——, who is present, turns to me:

"I do not think I shall need you any longer. Do not wait, but try and find your captain and the rest of your company."

(Censored.)

Hardly have we set out on the march, when a few shots sing over us. Quick volleying succeeds, until the crackling of rifles again covers the whole plain.

"They are starting again, Lieutenant," says Chabeau.

It is true; they are starting again, and, what is more, as hard as they are able to. "Fire on and always, my Boches," I murmur, "that is what you are best fitted for You dared attack us hand to hand and man to man, only under the cover of night, and even for that you paid dearly, as you well know!"

I catch sight of a line of men, some thirty or so, away to the left. They represent, apparently, all that survive of a section. They are moving swiftly forward, stooping instinctively beneath the hail of lead. At the head of them marches an officer, slim built, bearded, yet of boyish appearance. Is it not Porchon?

I strike across towards him with all speed. I am certain now it is no other than Porchon. And he also has seen me and is approaching me. He is the first to utter the very question on my own tongue:

"Do you know where the Captain is?"

"No! Are you also looking for him?"

"And you! Then let us march together, old fellow."

We range our men in skirmishing formation and set off. All the while the bullets are whistling and spattering about us. Chancing to turn my head to one side, I suddenly detect an officer, sitting, the sodden ground notwithstanding, in the middle of a field. As he catches my eye, he waves his arm. I have an idea that he is shouting to us, but the infernal noise prevents me hearing what he says. I take a few steps in his direction, unexpectedly to find it is the colonel. Turning to Por-chon I shout the news aloud:

"It is the Colonel, I am going to see what he wants . . . look after my men, will you? . . . you understand? . . . Take my men. . . . Can you hear me? . . . ."

He nods swiftly, turns and continues steadily on his way towards the rising, beyond which one can hear the noise of hard fighting.

Saluting, I present myself to the colonel.

"Second-Lieutenant of Reserve."

He nods, smiling, and glances towards a puddle metamorphosed temporarily into a muddy fountain by a bullet.

"Reserve—or the Line! Ah, well, I fear bullets take no heed of such distinctions!"

He stares at me long and fixedly, as if engaged in weighing my invisible merit in the scales, and then explains clearly and rapidly exactly what he expects of me.

"All my orderlies are busy on some mission or the other. I wish you to find, without loss of an instant, Colonel G——, commanding the brigade, and ask him, in my name, to send to me here as many men as he can possibly spare of the —th. Tell him we are in contact with enormous effectives, that our losses up to the present have been very heavy, so heavy, in fact, that I am afraid my regiment is no longer capable of holding on.

"He must be near Hill 281, a mile to the north of Marats-la-Petite. Do everything in your power to find him, not losing a second, and impress upon him how urgent is my necessity for immediate reinforcements."

"Very well, *mon* Colonel!"

With the bullets humming in my ears, I set out at a speed which sends the mud splashing all over me, from head to foot. The old sense of elation is upon me, impelling me forward, forgetful of the night's happenings, impervious to fatigue—I must find the commander of the brigade and obtain the assistance so desperately needed, from him. There is no room for other thought than that in my brain. Happily, I do not dwell on the weight of the responsibility thrust upon me in this unlooked-for fashion; my burning desire is to succeed in my mission nothing more.

I have already started away at a run when the colonel receives a bullet in the forearm. With his other arm, he imperatively motions to me to keep on my way.

Skirting the base of a steep slope, I pass through a fire zone where the bullets in hundreds, whining and shrilling, tear up the soil all about me. Then I encounter a group of men, standing at the foot of a tree. There is a dying officer in the centre, supported against the tree-bole. A glimpse I have of a dark blue tunic wide opened, of a shirt stained with bright blood. The wounded man's head sags heavily down to his shoulder, and in the whitened, tortured face, moist from fearful agony, I recognize my own major.

But I must not stay!

My heart is thundering within me; there is a sharp pain between my shoulders; there is a rending pain at the small of my back. And my legs! Every other minute violent cramp paralyses thighs or calves, sending me sprawling to the earth, where I lie gasping and panting for what seem eternities, striving to fight it back. My sodden clothes become almost fantastically heavy, and the weight is for ever increasing. To the very tips of my fingers I feel the irregular, violent pulsing of my arteries; my cloth-covered sword scabbard pricks my hand.

On the top of a rising alongside the road is a road-mender's hut. Behind it, a section of dismounted *chasseurs* is drawn up. It opens out into skirmishing order and sets off briskly and confidently for the scene of the fighting.

I take a steep declivity at full speed. Once or twice I fall full length in the mud. Another slope is negotiated in a sitting attitude. At the bottom of it I stumble, bruised from head to foot, into a little wood, where some soldiers stand, waiting orders, leaning on their rifles. Still more dismounted *chasseurs*! They too deploy, ascend the slope, and march unflinchingly into the inferno. The fight rages continuously behind me, as well as away to the left.

For the third time I encounter dismounted *chasseurs*, formed up in sections. And one after another these sections breast the rising ground, reach the summit, where for a moment they remain clean-cut and distinct against the sky, and then plunge downwards into the heart of the fight.

Another steep descent! I take it lying flat on my back, creating a veritable avalanche of stones and rubble. This deposits me in a well-sheltered, luxuriant little ravine. Almost irresistible is the desire that springs up in me to stretch myself full length among the fresh, fragrant grasses, to bathe my fevered face in the moisture, to lie still there and forget. . . . In a panic I force myself to my feet, afraid of losing grip!

A 77 drops neatly into the hollow and explodes at the bottom of it. I receive a tremendous and disconcerting shock, while about me fragments of steel and lead plough and tear up the earth.

In response to a command, some *chasseurs* suddenly appear at the edge of the ravine, and roll down exactly at the point where a few moments earlier I had descended. One of them jumps down, his legs quite stiff, blood trickling out of one of his boots from a smashed leg.

"How pale you are," says a second-lieutenant who comes up. "Are you wounded?"

"I don't think there is anything much the matter with me," I reply. "A bunch of shrapnel caught me in the knapsack fortunately."

The wounds of the injured soldier are dressed. A second man lies prone and still, a bullet through his brain.

Shells are hurrying over us now, carrying their shrill messages; a good number burst a little before us, and the echo of their harsh, metallic explosions is flung from one side of the ravine to the other. At each explosion huge, torn fragments of steel fly high above us across the sky. Columns of yellow smoke, dense and heavy, drift slowly through the still air, until they encounter the pines whose branches part and disperse them.

"Do you know where I can find Colonel G——?" I ask the *chasseur* lieutenant.

"Not exactly! Somewhere close at hand, I think. But the major will be able to inform you of his whereabouts."

I find the major to be quite a young man, tall, with an expression at once frank and resolute. He listens to my mission and says:

"That is quite all right. You will find the Colonel behind that wood there— at least he was there less than an hour ago. Some of the ——th are entrenched on that slope.

(Censored.)

.... "Go along, and good fortune go with you!" I am pretty well exhausted by this time. Only some internal exaltation sustains me. This hollow is endless . . . this hill steep beyond imagination! Up at the top some men are moving about and talking. I tell myself to run onwards . . . but all I can do for the moment is to rest on my sword and slowly drag one swollen foot after the other. The pain in my back has become intense. Nevertheless I must go on. One final effort and I shall have reached my destination. Onwards! . . .

(Censored.)

The men I totteringly approach have assumed the dimensions of giants. They possess enormous, unbalanced bodies; they are monstrosities who dance before my burning eyes. With a gentle, sustained power, the mud itself seems to draw me towards them.

Forward! . . . But I can no longer move forward. . . . The light is failing. . . . Ah, what an unfortunate devil I am!

Someone raises and carries me with strong, careful arms. The sensation is good. Then some burning liquid scorches my mouth and throat, and instantly causes me to open my eyes. Close to my face, a voice asks:

"How do you feel now?"

"It is nothing at all," I say weakly. "Fatigue! no sleep . . . nothing to eat. Been fighting all night. It is all right!"

I am lying in a trench covered with muddy straw. Near me is a lieutenant and several men. It is the former who just spoke to me and who presses whiskey upon me from his flask.

I look at the collar of his coat and see the number of the regiment I have been seeking.

"Ah! So I have found you," I cried. "Is the whole regiment here?"

The abruptness of my question takes him back for a moment.

"Yes, that is so! Didn't you know?"

"I should say I didn't, seeing that I have zigzagged all over the countryside for you and Colonel G——. We hadn't the slightest idea where to find you at the advance post and for hours we, unsupported, have been at grips with more Germans than you could count in a week.

"You are wanted very badly indeed over there. Do you know where he is—Colonel G——?"

"In this wood, I believe. He has taken up his position somewhere before those batteries you can hear firing. It should be possible to see him from here."

He raises himself and looks about.

"I can see him no longer, but he has been here for a long time past. They will certainly be able to tell you over there where he is gone."

I thank him and ask before leaving: "Just one more drop of '*Gniole*,' if you can spare it. I am very badly in want of a stiffener."

I take a long gulp of neat spirit and set off towards the 75's which are growling together in the wood.

When I reach them I find the artillerymen absolutely overjoyed. They are working their guns at a speed and with a precision and enthusiasm which greatly impresses an infantryman such as I am. One has scarcely time to perceive the small copper shells which are gallantly waging their part in this long distance duel. They pass before the eyes in a thin line, red and yellow, instantly to vanish into the breech, still smoking from the last shot. And the next second the gun hurls its shrapnel message with a report imperious and gay as though delighting in the glory of the spurting flame and the heavy smoke drifting away in a column.

The artillerymen run, jump and gesticulate about their gun. Most of them have flung aside their coats and rolled their sleeves to their elbows. They are one and all in high spirits, joking and laughing boyishly. With my mudstained clothes, with my pale and lugubrious face, my advent has an effect similar to that of an owl suddenly alighting in the midst of a flock of sparrows. But their happiness is contagious, and little by little I feel my own spirits rising. They give me the impression that something happy has occurred. I question a lieutenant who is marking the fall of the shells through his glasses, shaking from head to foot the while from excitement.

"Things going well? Eh?"

He turns towards me. The joy which fills him is plainly legible in his face. He laughs exuberantly:

"I should say they are going well. The Germans are giving way— deserting their positions like rats a sinking ship."

He laughs once more. "Listen to our 75's! They are making them dance like madmen! That is the way to carry on, what? They are being kicked in the sterns now, the swine!"

A staff captain on foot is watching the delighted gunners. He laughs also and repeats several times in a loud voice: "Good! Very good!"

I approach him and in a few words inform him of what was befalling half an hour ago over towards Vauxmarie on the Erize road. I repeat to him my wounded colonel's words, indicate the course I have followed, express my joy at having finally reached my destination, and add:

"I should, however, like to see Colonel G——, as I have been sent to him."

The captain pauses before he replies kindly:

"You go and get some rest now. The ——th are no longer needed. Nor will you be wanted for a little while. You have done well."

Then he informs me that my regiment has been withdrawn from the firing line and is being re-established a little to the rear. On his map he indicated the point of assembly and afterwards shakes me warmly by the hand.

"*Aurevoir*, young man," he says. "Sleep well, eat well, keep yourself fit. You will want all your strength to keep fast on the heels of the Boches."

My heart leaps within me.

"Then, Captain, we have won a great victory?"

"I do not know . . . not yet. But truly it will be so if all our rascals have progressed since Sunday as these have."

A surge of joy sweeps through me—a curious warmth, sweet, fervent and strong. Oh, that this may be true, that it may be true! The nervous tension under which I have laboured for hours past breaks suddenly. I feel strangely small and weak, and am obsessed by an insane desire to cry without constraint.

In the background, the 75's aligned along the edge of the wood continue joyously their triumphant salvoes. But the rattle they make now sounds queerly afar off, as though my head had been enveloped in a thick hood of wadding. Beneath my feet the soil, strewn with wet pine needles, becomes elastic, enabling me to walk without effort. And so I leave the captain, walking slowly, already forgetful of my recent travails, blind to the things about me.

Visions of those who are dear to me dance before my eyes, I can see them as though in life smiling tenderly upon me. They give me a sense of being protected, watched over, soothed. I can even hear their familiar voices speaking rather solemnly but caressingly, nevertheless.

"Be of good heart. It is only the passage of the cruel moments such as those of yesterday, of today, and maybe those of tomorrow which, bringing victory, shall reunite us."

(*Censored.*)

Before rejoining my regiment I have to pass along a road leading from one of the Marats to the other. Near Marats-la-Petite I discover a first-aid post, and show the surgeon my back, which has become still more painful. The post consists of a dimly-lit barn, containing several seriously wounded men lying on straw. One could scarcely distinguish the outlines of their bodies and could only hear their groans emanating from the gloom. The floor was littered with pieces of cotton wool stained with blood, dried and brown, or freshly crimson.

"You must rest," the surgeon told me. "The shrapnel has not penetrated, but you have some really famous bruises."

I discovered my regiment bivouacked in a meadow near a stone culvert bestriding a large ditch full of water.

Porchon is there, also the captain.

(*Censored.*)

Of the 5th Company there survive about 50 men only. And only a few more of the 6th. Not a single officer remains. They were stationed further ahead than we were that night, and the darkness, the confusion, the rain, enabled the Boches to enfilade their trenches, marked during the day by those large aeroplanes with the black crosses. It was a white-handed massacre, the disgusting exploit of assassins who stab in the back.

The Germans in question belonged to the 13th Army Corps, and were for the most part Würtembergers. They had been made drunk with alcohol and ether—such at least the prisoners had avowed. In the knapsacks of some of them were found incendiary pastilles, and many of my men assured me that they had seen a number of Germans burst into flame from head to foot when struck by a bullet, and continue to burn like torches.

A march across inundated fields or over roads whose puddles reflect the wan sky. I walk in the rear of the company with the captain, who moves onwards with long, slow steps, his inevitable lance marking time against the pebbles. Two prisoners march alongside us. The captain, a man of Lorraine, from the neighbourhood of Sarrebourg, gossips with one of them, I with the other. He is a gardener from Esslingen, near Stuttgart. I chat with him about these towns which I know well. A certain confidence having been established between us, he offers me his tin of meat. I accept it without exhibition of much pride; it is certain he will be given something to eat tomorrow, and as for us, maybe we shall get nothing. I divide the booty with my orderly and two of my men. It was excellent, that meat, surrounded with a transparent jelly. . . . (*Censored*) . . . Bread is lacking, but that does not matter. The meat suffices to fill a void.

Halt at the edge of a wood on a slope. Dead leaves from last autumn still lie about, and here and there are some quite freshly yellow which the convulsion of the night has stripped from the branches.

As company after company comes up the men hail one another, laughing and congratulating themselves on having escaped. Sitting amid the undergrowth, they eat what they have got. Those who have been wise enough to preserve at the bottom of their knapsacks a tin of meat have become kings. The others roam about in their vicinity, tortured by a covetousness which is plain in their eyes, burning with a desire to commandeer, yet not daring so far. Fortunate, too, beyond their fellows are those who have found in the knapsacks of captured Germans small sweetened biscuits. Many men raid the fields, returning with carrots and terrific turnips which they cut up with their pocket-knives and swallow voraciously.

A night dull and cold. Lying on the bare earth of the slope, I am constantly freezing. The stones which form my bed penetrate my flesh and make me as uncomfortable as if I had as many wounds. A nightmare haunts me. It concerns the loss of my flask by one of my men who should have brought it to me filled with water, but whom I cannot find anywhere. Deeply do I regret having teased Porchon because he left his sword among the straw of his trench, while I contrived to save mine! I have my sword, I have my cap, I have my knapsack, but no longer have I my flask. And that is a loss that renders the future dark and gloomy. Still sleeping, I recall the exquisite taste of the few drops of tepid water I swallowed that night at Sommaisne, which were as balm to my arid, burning throat; I recall the spirit I gulped that very morning, and which built up anew my declining strength ... no longer a flask! What a misfortune!

Friday, September 11th.

"Attention! Fall in!"

We depart. Ten or so "marmites" burst behind us over a wood not very far away. The Boches must have smelt us hidden beneath the trees. There is just as much water in the fields as yesterday—puddles, pools forming miniature lakes, and microscopical rivers running between upstanding ridges.

We encounter more woods and lose our way among the dense growth, vividly green by reason of the recent rain. We stumble through ditches, grass-choked, and thrust a way through interlacing brambles which push their shoots into the middle of the path. From the heart of the wood ring out monotonously the sharp trilling and twittering of many birds at song. Occasionally, a blackbird rises and flies before us, but so low that it is almost able to touch the earth with its claws; in the breeze its wings create the leaves rise and flutter. Above our heads a break in the clouds forms a lake, blue, limpid and deep. All is stillness and peace.

But when we leave the wood the world has become grey and depressing. We splash across a marshy field in which guns and ammunition wagons are drawn up, plastered with mud to the axles, and tarnished with splashes. There are the entrails and soft skins of sheep lying in little round piles in the puddles. Bones are scattered about, to which fragments of rain-washed meat are still attached, and they serve to give the bare field the semblance of a *charnel*-house. A road crosses it, shining with stagnant water and bordered until lost to sight by dejected-looking trees. And over this unelevating prospect, leaden rain-laden clouds hang low and drift one into the other, until the little lake of blueness is completely veiled from view.

We are at Rosnes. It is a village alongside the road. It serves to make me think rather pathetically of all those houses which have not yet suffered bombardment, of those barns even, which contain hay, hay soft and fragrant, in which one can find warmth and comfort.

We leave Rosnes behind us and, marching easy, slowly ascend a steep rising, finally to arrive on a plateau covered far and near with thick growth. The breeze passing over it gives it the appearance of a mysterious and noisome pond whose icy surface is ruffled by autumn winds.

At Captain C——'s invitation, a meeting of officers takes place. It is he who, at Gercourt, distributed the men of our detachment into companies. And now here he commands the regiment, since the colonel and the chief of the first battalion are wounded, and those of the second and third are killed. It is only then I learn that for several days past the 3rd Battalion has been commanded by the officer of *gendarmerie* whom I saw on the morning of the 9th, when he ran up shouting at us and at our major because he hesitated to throw us out over a bare plain swept by machine-gun fire. He had died magnificently.

Captain C—— addressed us in his unimpassioned voice. He congratulated us and told us he relied on each one of us. We were worn out, but it was necessary to keep going and preserve appearances before the men, in order to maintain their courage so long as the present hare times continued; to prevent them, by the exhibition of our own energy and enthusiasm, from succumbing to the temptation of grumbling and complaining.

From the expression of the faces about me, from the serenity legible in each man's eyes, I gathered we were all ready to face the future, whatsoever it might contain. It almost seemed we leaned on each other for support, true brothers by the common faith within us. A grace exalted and fortified us.

Thus my captain became my battalion chief and Porchon my company commander. I was well content, because the passage of each day had brought Porchon and myself nearer each other. I know him today to be a man open and frank to the last word, ambitious to show himself just, but indulgent in all things, and brave with that simplicity which exalts courage.

Moreover, I love his good humour, his never failing laugh, the ardent life in him. To be gay and light-hearted, to remain so under the sharpest physical sufferings, even when devastation and cruel death break or snatch away the men or human things about you; to remain constant before these assaults which strike more at the heart than at the intellect, is for a leader a hard but sacred duty. Porchon had perhaps taught me this. No longer did I wish to deaden my senses in order to render my task the easier. I was eager to confront all :he demands of this prodigious and unnatural world into which I had been suddenly cast; I no longer even sought to escape those duties which seem to lead one to certain death. And these things would be easy to achieve if only I could attain something of that good humour which I sedulously sought to possess as one sets out to conquer a virtue. Porchon would assist me.

We set off together to settle the location of the trenches which our company must construct. Our men set to work with tools obtained from a park. The picks quickly break up the brown, heavy soil. It is raining, but the task is not difficult. The men sing and jokes fly about—probably because the first section has already been called up for the distribution of rations!

They have descended towards Seigneulles, a village close at hand at the bottom of the valley. From our position we can see the regimental carts pointing their shafts towards us, tilted and supported on garden fences. Further away, emerging from a lake of greenness, is a small group of houses, and the cock on a church steeple.

Soon now along the roadside the fires begin to smoke. This evening we are going to eat cooked meat and hot potatoes. We shall have straw for our beds and a roof to shelter us from the wind and rain. Who cares for tomorrow since life today is so good!

Saturday, September 12th. Heavily and dreamlessly I sleep, and awake to find myself in precisely the same attitude as that in which I flung myself down the preceding night. The straw wraps me in grateful warmth, rather moist, perhaps, because the water in my saturated clothes has evaporated during the night. Above me I can see the rafters of the roof from which dusty spider-webs hang; for the moment I am amazed to find myself thus snugly ensconced beneath a roof, instead of the usual branches or the bare sky to which I have become accustomed. The rain trickles softly and gently over the tiles. The sound intensifies my sense of comfort, and it pleases me to think that I have slept in warmth and comfort, despite the never-ceasing downpour.

But the rain exacts its revenge in the course of the day. For duty compels us once more to climb up to the plateau to complete the trenches commenced the day before. We find that in the night the torrent has well-nigh filled them with liquid mud. Some sappers, however, come to our assistance, and, thanks to them, we are able to shelter ourselves from the worst of the downpour; they hastily construct a thick roof of baulks of timber covered with earth.

The men work easily, flinging jests one to the other. The incidents of the night attack are revived and acquire a totally new force by reason of the simple words in which they are related.

"I was all right at the beginning," says Martigny, one of my men. "But all at once, while I was still firing, down toppled a Boche right on top of me, without so much as a 'by your leave!' I was on my knees and he lay across my calves. It's not easy to fire in such a position as that! Little by little the weight forced my knees down into the mud; the water rose almost up to my hands: how was I to refill my magazine? I could not see the animal, but you can take my word for it, he was heavy."

And a second:

"A good job for me that I was once fencing- sergeant in the regulars! Otherwise I should not be here now. Not even time to fix my bayonet before I found one of the ugly pigs on top of me with his skewer. I thought to myself: 'What's all this about? But you are going to find you can joke once too often, my Boche!' And there we were all in and at it. I parried a thrust with the stock of my rifle, but what sort of defence could I put up, seeing that my weapon was much shorter than his? Only he didn't manage to get his bayonet into me! . . . There wasn't even a cartridge! I tell you that Boche kept me jumping from side to side until I felt like dying from weariness. You know what a job it is to parry, when you can no longer feel your own fingers? Still jumping, I said to myself: 'What in the name of glory are those asses right and left footling about? Are they going to stand by and see me knocked out?' Oh! but they were there all right, and it was Gillet to the right who put a bullet into him while he was pausing to take a breath. Then I stuck on my bayonet and filled my magazine. There were others still coming up, you understand!"

"Sons of pigs, these Boches!" rasps a miner from the North. "And what mugs they are too, *Mon Dieu*! When I saw them swarming over towards me, 'Martin,' said I to myself, 'you're done for this time!' And then: 'Hurrah!' they're off! Bang, bang, bang! And I knew no more."

"Martin, you are babbling," grunts a huge Champenois, who is smoking his pipe and listening with eyes atwinkle. "Hammer away at the earth, seeing that is what you were born for; but don't mix yourself up in conversations, because you can't talk."

He spits on his hands, rubs them against each other, and taking up his pick starts digging again with long, steady, powerful strokes.

Eight o'clock in the morning and nothing before us but a day of rest. We do not go down to the village, however, until four o'clock in the afternoon. Then we hastily erect temporary shelters against the weather, building them of pointed stakes, branches and bundles of straw. The rain sweeps down obliquely, driven by a westerly wind. Men lie face down in the straw through which course streams of rain. Many of them fall asleep, and when they wake after their short *siesta*, the straw has left on their cheek; crimson furrows which look like scars.

The plateau, covered as it now is with little huts of straw erected in less than an hour, has all the appearance of a gipsy encampment. The captain's stick thrust in the ground before one of the larger of these shelters indicates Headquarters. He's pretty certain to be there himself, although there are no signs either of him or of his messengers. Through the rain-mist, indistinct figures occasionally drift across the deserted plain without giving it life. The rain makes them vague, colourless, almost formless. Gradually they draw away into indistinctness, finally to disappear so abruptly as to leave one puzzled and mystified. A second before they were visible; they are no longer so now; and there remains only the drenched plain on which our straw huts appear like strange unhealthy excrescences.

Between two showers, Porchon appears before me. He carries in his hand a can in which there is something smoking and steaming. He offers it to me with a plainly self-satisfied grin.

"A fine company, mine, what? Everything in stock you can possibly want. Smell that, old man, and fill your nostrils well before drinking it."

To my amazement the contents of the can prove to be cocoa, which duly disappears. I can recall nothing since leaving the depot which has tended to create such a sense of comfort within me, such a sense of well-being, security and peace. Can we indeed be at war? Can one reconcile the thought of war with steaming, boiling cocoa? My astonishment lasts longer than the fragrant liquid.

"Where did you find that? . . ." I asked.

Without replying he draws from his large pockets a brandy flask, a sausage and two pots of jam from Bar-le-Duc. These jams gave the show away.

"I know!" I exclaimed. "You've run across a peddling grocer from Bar?"

And while speaking, a vision I had often seen on the roads at home comes to me, and I add with a tone of deep conviction:

"He had a little wagon with oilcloth curtains, and there were bells on the horse's collar."

Porchon's eyes opening wide told me I had guessed correctly . . . . (*Censored*) . . . . : "

In the evening we go into the village. I stroll slowly towards the barn where my section is billeted. In the square, a group of noisy soldiers is gathered before a house which has nothing in particular to distinguish it from its neighbours. With much pushing and stretching of necks they are contriving to scan a big placard stuck on the wall. Of course, I can't be left out when there's something to be seen, though actuated by nothing but sordid curiosity.

The first word that encounters my eyes, however, gives me a violent shock. I can see nothing else but that word, which instantly seizes upon my excited imagination and seems to presage things marvellous, superhuman, incredible. The word is:

"Victory!"

It sings in my ears, that word. It echoes through all the streets, it bursts on me like a triumphant fanfare.

"Victory!" Thrills pass through me, enthusiasm seizes upon me and stirs me so violently as to make me feel almost sick. I feel that I am too small to contain the emotion to which the sacred word gives rise.

The retreat of the 1st, 2nd and 3rd German Armies is becoming pronounced before our left and centre. In its turn, the enemy's 4th Army is beginning to fall back to the north of Vitry and Sermaize.

So that is it, then! We have been progressing everywhere. We have grappled with them, badly-torn them, wounded them! Oh! that it may run and run, that German blood, until every particle of strength shall have streamed out of them! . . .

In the light of this news other things become simple and clear to me. That endless retreat of the first days of September, those forced marches through the heat along dusty, stifling roads—were not the flight of a disordered army knowing itself defeated. A retreat, yes; but step by step, and not an inch further than a line agreed upon by our leaders. Beside this bulletin announcing victory, I find the proclamation issued by the *generalissimo* the night before the battle:

The moment is come when we must no longer look behind us. . . . It is time now to attack and drive back the enemy. . . .

That that was so every man among us had felt and known instinctively.

Die where you stand rather than give way.

No one had read those words aloud to us at Condé in that hour when we turned once more and faced north. But they had been in our hearts; they had become our purpose in life and our will. Not knowing that on the events of those days of durance depended the safety of the country, we had nevertheless made the terrible but necessary sacrifice lightheartedly, joyously.

Since those days, our land had been drenched with blood wherever we had loaded our rifles or fixed our bayonets. The fragile wall of living flesh had defied their enormous shells; their bullets could not shatter it; and when, after an avalanche of steel, the helmeted hordes had rushed forward to trample it beneath their feet, not all their stubborn attacks, renewed again and again with desperate fury throughout five long days, succeeded in creating the breach for which they had sacrificed so much.

Today, over towards Vauxmarie, the sappers are gathering together the bodies of the fallen Boches lying as thickly strewn as the grass in the fields. The corpses are taken in tens in tumbrils towards huge pits, yawning to receive their loads of dead flesh. When the carts arrive at the edge of these graves, they are tilted up, and the bodies tumble out, arms and legs swinging horribly, grotesquely. And the good earth of France swiftly hides from sight those greenish uniforms, those decomposing faces with blinded eyes, those heavy nailed boots which never again will trample the soil of our beloved land.

A sapper coming fresh from this scene of horror, unable to rid himself of the soul-sickening memory of it, gave me these details. His words bring images before my eyes which remain with me until they assume the form of almost an hallucination. Yet nevertheless the gruesome picture awakens in me something of a bitter pride, a fierce joy—I feel an uncontrollable desire to shout aloud, a desire to kill still so imperious that I have to clench my teeth to repress it.

It was as I stood before the little low-roofed mayor's house in the village, my eyes scanning those few lines written by some surgeon or other, that I became the prey of one of the most intense and confusing emotions it is possible for the human heart to experience.

Several times I walked up and down, passing and repassing soldiers still hustling one another in their endeavours to read the announcements. Strangely alike in appearance were they. The faces of one and all were mud-stained and bristles filled the hollows of their cheeks. Their blue great-coats bore traces of the dust of the road, of the mud of the fields, of the heavy rain; their boots and gaiters had long since acquired a permanently sombre colour; their clothes were worn and torn at knees and elbows, and from their tattered sleeves protruded hands incredibly dirty and hardened. Most of them appeared wearied and wretched beyond description. Nevertheless, these were the men who had just fought with superhuman energy, who had proved themselves stronger than German bullets and bayonets; these men were the conquerors.

I should have liked to have told each one of them of the sudden glow of affection which filled me for them—those soldiers who have now won the admiration and respect of the whole world by sacrificing themselves so grandly without thought of sacrifice, without realizing the depth of their heroism. Tomorrow perhaps they must once again take up their knapsacks, fasten on once more those cartridge-belts which chafe the shoulders, and go marching for hours, despite feet that swell and burn; sleep beside ditches full of water, eating only when the occasion presents, knowing hunger sometimes and thirst and coldness. They will go on, and among them not one will be found to grumble at the life before them.

And when the hour sounds to fight once again, they will shoulder their rifles with the same easy indifference, will rush forward as eagerly between the bursts of enemy fire, will display the same tenacity before the mightiest efforts of the enemy. For in them dwell souls, ever scornful of weakness, strengthened and fortified by the conviction of victory, capable of conquering physical pain and weariness. Oh, all of you, my brothers in arms, we are going to do still better than we have already done, are we not?

Cries ring out from the end of the village. Men begin to run as fast as they can towards the plateau. What can be happening—where are they going? Suddenly I understand. Up there on the plateau I perceive a swarm of soldiers, numbering half a battalion, perhaps. The colours of their coats and trousers are remarkably fresh, blue and red; mess-tins and water flasks shimmer and gleam brightly, despite the poorness of the light. These men, in fact, are exactly as they should be for parade; they are fresh and spick and span. They are newly-arrived reinforcements.

Happy men, to come to war in a moment of victory, not to know the agony of retreat before a blow has been struck, a retreat which no one can explain! The vision of the Cuisy trenches, of a sunlit field of fire, has never for a moment ceased to be with me during all the days before Sommaisne. We had to retreat and we knew not why! Happy men indeed who come to christen their weapons amid the intoxication of a pursuit, without having had first to suffer the torture of a disaster such as we suffered!

5

Behind the Crown Prince's Army

Sunday, September 13th.

We are probably leaving Seigneulles today," the captain said to me
a short while ago; "let us hope we are not going to be kept constantly
on the move again."

That hope is fervent within me, captain! Meanwhile, what spirit
of evil tempted me to eat all day long yesterday? Those eggs which
a quartermaster of the 5th gave me were so deliciously fresh that I
pricked two holes in the shells and ate them raw. Most luscious, too,
were the contents of the gunners' frying-pan! Tender and roasted to
perfection the fowl of which the captain offered me a wing; plump
the rabbit my "fags" gently simmered over a slow fire behind our barn.
But alas! what a night I spent!

The straw pricked my hands and face and feet; it was so burningly
hot, too, that I yearned for the freshness of soft sheets. I was feverish.
My stomach felt as heavy as a huge lump of lead. At times it was seized
with strange palpitations; at others, it became as an India-rubber ball,
inflated to the last degree. When I dozed, nightmares peopled the
night, awakening me with such a start that I bumped my head against
the staves of a gigantic tub behind which I had fixed up my bed of
straw. By the time the morning came, I felt able to sleep a little, but
with the broad light of day streaming in through the open door of the
barn, there remained nothing else to do but to get up and dress. Legs
feeble, mouth pasty, head void! What a triple fool I had been! And here
I am with nothing before me but long marches!

Still, why complain when it is my own fault? I am not yet dead of
indigestion, and tomorrow it will be gone!

I dip my nose in the miniature basin lent to Porchon and myself by
the village doctor. I do not know in what kind of a basin the amiable

doctor himself washes, but the one he has lent us is farcical. To dissolve the grime of a week's accumulation would alone necessitate buckets and buckets of water; and all we have is a few drops of cold water at the bottom of a pot about as big as a thimble, and our washing has to be done in a saucer. Happily, my orderly appears while I am still wallowing in the midst of my woes, bearing a camp pail filled to overflowing. I splash about to my heart's content, indifferent to the fate of the floor, which is generously watered. My nocturnal discomforts are soon forgotten. I feel better and am well content.

We depart at noon. My section is drawn up before the barn, each man with his pack on his back, his rifle grounded. No one is missing. I inspect them to find that they have all brushed their uniforms, washed and shaved. No speck of dust on either equipment or boots. Heads are erect, eyes clear, everything, in fact, most pleasing and satisfactory.

A peculiar silence invariably prevails during the last seconds before setting off on the march. It did so on the present occasion, until it was shattered by a sudden outburst of rifle fire in the distance. What can that be? Is it a joke? For since the day before yesterday, we have not even heard a single shell.

"Lieutenant, Lieutenant! Do you see it?"

Every man peers into the sky in the direction indicated by one of them. I can see it now, a Taube, small, clear and distinct against a cloudless patch of sky, flying directly towards us. We know their silhouettes well by now, and though only the hum of the engine betrays an almost invisible speck, it is not long before we call out "Boche" or "French."

There is no question about this being Boche, and they must be firing upon it from Rosnes or Marats-la-Grande. It is quite out of our range; all we can do is to stand and watch. Nevertheless, every one of the men is positively trembling from eagerness to chance a shot. One of them, in fact, goes so far as to raise and aim his rifle, and then, half-turning towards me:

"May I, Lieutenant, may I?"

"Don't be a fool, Godard!" I reply rather severely. "What! Fire at it from here!"

In a hard school I have learnt to know the price of a cartridge, as well as a horror of waste!

Some man in an adjoining section suddenly cries triumphantly:

"They have got it!"

It is true the aeroplane has oscillated a little, a very little—but it is quite sufficient to send the men dancing with joy and shouting from sheer delight as if they were children. As for myself, I am only too certain that we have by no means "got it." It is still flying quite steadily. For an instant the whole fuselage is visible; then nothing but the tops of its wings are showing. In turning, it banks steeply and remains suspended for a moment before vanishing from sight behind the roof of our barn. For the men, that is sufficient. They are one and all convinced that it has fallen, that it has crashed to the earth, there away towards the north. I don't mind them believing it!

Forward! We march slowly across fields which are still heavy, but which are no longer puddles, so at least we are able to keep our feet dry. Ahead, the 8th begins to straggle, falls out of line and gets in our way. Each time we pass an orchard, men fall out, run to the trees, and fill their knapsacks with apples and quinces. On such occasions I growl out:

"Fall in, confound you! . . ."

Finally, however, it becomes necessary for me to drop on two or three of the looters, whom I compel to throw down their gatherings at the foot of the tree they have robbed. One must occasionally adopt forcible expedients to preserve some semblance of order.

Marats-la-Grande. We do not pass through the village. Some mounted batteries are passing and scaling the sloping fields towards the road. The riders are shouting and whipping their horses, already straining at the collar. Poor beasts! So thin that one can count their ribs, sides chafed raw by the harness, heads hanging, they strain and strain until their laboured breathing is audible, while their large bleared eyes speak eloquently of their sufferings.

A grave; two posts have been tied to form a cross! On the horizontal one a deep notch has been made with a knife, revealing the white heart of the wood. Someone has written in pencil the name of the soldier whose body is lying in the earth, his uniform for his shroud. The number of his regiment, his company and the date of his death, the 9th of September, are also inscribed. Four days! Only four days ago that decomposing something lying beneath the mound of earth was a man in the full flood of life, hoping, perhaps, soon to be reunited to the dear ones waiting for him. Four days! . . . His parents would not have heard yet.

More graves. They are not laid out in any particular order, or even in groups. At irregular intervals, they line the road we are following, which is no more than a trampled-down track over fresh grass between trees in leaf. Everywhere one can see these sad little crosses, on almost all of which a red cap hangs. Without halting, the men read aloud the inscriptions. The 8th of September, the 9th of September, the 10th of September. . . .

And here is one which is not marked with the little cross of branches. A stake has been simply driven into the ground, bearing a burnt-in inscription to tell passers-by the name of the dead man; on the newly-turned earth some white stones have been arranged in the form of a cross—they seem to protect him who lies there better and more intimately.

Hastily-made graves, turned out with small trenching tools, how I wish you were much deeper! Your lines suggest the shape of the body you hide from our eyes. The rain must have soaked you these last days and nights! But at least calm and peace are with you. The enemy is far away, never to return. Guard well, then, your poor dead, until the day dawns when the old men and women shall come to demand of you the bodies of their loved ones!

We march onwards a few minutes longer and reach a bare plain studded with shell-craters. The sun is sinking, the rays of its golden light striking obliquely. Mutilated horses are lying about, their stiff legs crossed or thrust up towards the sky. Their swollen sides betray the work of putrefaction within. A viscous fluid trickles from the corners of their mouths, which reveal their long yellow teeth; their bluish eyes have become filmy and liquid. They are a revolting, nauseating spectacle! I recognize the sickly, penetrating stench which always becomes more pronounced with the approach of night and is invariably associated with the corpses of big animals.

"Halt!" Before us is a line of trenches covered with straw. It is near here I fell on the morning of the 10th, and the men who picked me up sheltered me beneath a roof similar to this one. The atmosphere of human residence is still perceptible. Its occupants cannot have been gone long.

Rest, a prelude to settling down for the night. A final snack: the jams from Bar emerge from our knapsacks. The men are swarming over the plain. I watch a few of them dragging behind them some disreputable red eiderdowns which are shedding their feathers; others are carrying pieces of oilcloth picked up Heaven knows where; and some have become the proud possessors of dirty coverlets full of holes.

Where on earth are they going? Two of them who were just strolling between the pyramids of rifles have suddenly disappeared as though they had dived from the camp. There must be a steep slope there with some farm, or perhaps a village, at the bottom of it. Looters have noses like bloodhounds for inhabited spots, and start at once in pursuit. There is no cure for that disease. I study my map to find that we are just above Erize-la-Grande. Its road and houses cannot be a hundred yards from where I am. I dispatch a non-com. in pursuit of the men, with orders to bring them back at once. I leave the wet trench to walk a little in the open air before the fall of night.

A few cyclists go by, rather more elegant than ourselves, in their short coats, knee-breeches and their *puttees*. Swinging from their belts are Boche flasks covered with a cloth coloured similarly to the uniforms we have so often seen. I regret my own lost flask and envy the cyclists. I have recognized the man of the 5th to whom I entrusted it, but that does not carry me much further, although I have made a mental note of him for a future occasion. "Fall in!"

New orders have just arrived and we are to move on again.

Before leaving, I pick up a fragment of shell over which I stumbled. It is fifty centimetres long by fifteen wide, with jagged edges like the teeth of a saw. I contemplate this terrible thing lying heavy in my hand. To what kind of a shell, swift and growling, must it have belonged? This fragment must be one of those which cleanly sweep away an arm or leg, tear off a head, or cut a man completely in two. And holding it thus in my hand, heavy and cold, I remember a poor little cyclist who was killed close to us in Septsarges Wood—one leg taken away at the hip and the lower part of his abdomen laid open.

Trees and a shimmer of green on a wide road, away to the north. Night is falling. Suddenly through the greyness we find ourselves looking upon some ruins—we have reached Erize-la-Petite.

The entrance to the village, which is indeed little more than a hamlet, was choked with carriages, with ploughs and horse-rakes, which had been drawn to one side. In silence we pass before the shattered houses. Nothing remains but the mere shells of walls and distorted chimneys still standing above the wrecked hearths. Some charred beams have rolled almost into the middle of the roadway; a large mechanical mowing-machine raises its broken shaft like a stump.

The regiment defiles through the gloomy evening; our steps resound lugubriously and violate the surrounding desolation. In a short while, when the last section will have disappeared over the summit of the hill, the cold and silent night will descend again on the village, and peace shroud the poor, dead houses.

For the last time I turn and look back, glutting my eyes with this vision of desolation. Then I resume mechanically the onward march, sad to the point of tears, with the wan chillness of death in my heart.

Another road skirting the line which links Rembercourt with Vauxmarie and Beauzée. In the ditches, hunched up or stretched at full length, are human corpses. A single corpse is a rare spectacle. As a rule they are lying huddled together as if seeking to warm each other. The failing light reveals blue coats and red trousers; Frenchmen; more Frenchmen, in fact nothing but Frenchmen! Judge my enthusiasm on finding some Boches among them! I fall out several times to make sure that these really are Boches. The foe cannot have had the time to hide away that lot!

The night becomes black and corpses are no longer visible. But they are always there, at the bottom of the ditches, on the slopes at the very edge of the road. We realize their presence even in the dark. By shielding the eyes and peering hard, it is possible to see the eerie heaps which have lost all resemblance to that of which they are made. Beyond all, one can smell them; the peculiar, indescribable stench is heavy in the still evening air. The slowly moving breeze passing over those bodies fills our noses and throats with the odour. It makes us shudder instinctively, fearful lest that welter of putrefaction should be communicated from them to us.

Not a word in the ranks; nothing but the regular tramp, tramp, before and behind me; occasionally someone coughs, a little dryly, or a man spits. That is all. It must be cold, yet my head and hands are burning, and my will struggles to subdue an uncontrollable inclination to turn to my right where the cool waters of the Aire, flowing by the roadside, are betrayed by the stagnant pools under the trees.

An unexpected halt! The men bump their noses against the packs of the file in front. Confusion and much swearing. Then quick commands:

"Quartermasters prepare rations for distribution."

It is the best of all signs. The day's march is ended. Yet for an hour we are kept waiting on the road. The stench is worse than ever. There are dead horses somewhere near here.

Deuxnoux-devant-Beauzée. We pass in turn before the ration-carts. By the light of swinging lanterns I catch a glimpse of a bearded face, the blade of a butcher's knife, at the end of a bare forearm, quarters of meat, and the twinkling buttons of a greatcoat. The lantern dances on its way; nothing remains but confused, restless forms.

Very soon, however, fires are leaping and glowing in the roadway outside the houses. The cooks are bending over them, their weather-hardened, highly coloured faces thrown into relief, while the gigantic shadows they cast flit along the walls.

We mess in the house of a farmer's wife whose husband is on service. This time last night she was waiting on German officers. She showed us a plate containing the remains of some pickled cabbage, and exclaims:

"See, *messieurs*, they left such a lot behind them!"

She soon gets to work, and, propping a loaf against her ample bosom, cuts off thick slices of new bread (new bread, mark you!). In another moment our glasses are merry with cider brought from the cellar in a stone jug at least two feet high

"But are you quite sure," she asks, "that they won't return?"

I reply to her in a fashion that pleases her:

"Madam, you can bet your own child's cap upon it!"

We are well abed when there sounds a heavy knocking on the door of the barn, which my men have already firmly closed.

"Pannechon! Pannechon! Come out, *mon vieux*!"

Pannechon is my orderly. I hear him emerging from the hay and stumbling over sleepers who do not scruple to tell him what they think of him.

Then the door opens creakingly. Pouf! . . . What a smell! It seems to be compounded of skim-milk, rats, perspiration, and other indescribable things. It is sharp and nauseous, and quite turns me. What on earth can smell so vilely? All at once the stench revives an old memory; brings back to my mind the picture of one of the Boche "assistant's" rooms at the Lakanal Lyceum. I used to go there from time to time to wile away an hour or so, and, at the same time, to acquire fluency in his language. This was in the course of a remarkably hot summer, and he used to take off his coat and vest and put himself at his ease, so that when I opened the door that same stench struck me in the face, seized me by the throat, as it were. He used to grin, half of his fatuous face hidden by tortoise-shell spectacles and greet me with his heavy, guttural tones:

"*Mon Ongle Penchamin*! Splendeed, splendeed! And so teepigally Vrench!"

I remember I used to push my chair as far back as possible, until, in fact, my back was against the wall, and finish up by saying:

"Let us go out into the park, shall we? We shall be able to breathe better out there than here."

Ah, well! Destiny decrees that I shall now sleep amidst this oppressive smell of Germans, stretched out on the hay in which they have sheltered. Bah! . . . It's a dear price to pay for recovery of possession!

"Pannechon! What on earth's this?"

I seize the corner of a piece of cloth protruding from the straw. I pull it out and find it to be a greyish-green mantle with a red collar.

"Pannechon, pitch that outside!"

I stretch myself out, cover myself with my greatcoat and close my eyes. "Hullo! What is this poking my side!"

I thrust my hand into the hay and feel something hard with many corners. Patient investigation reveals a lacquered toilet-box with a mirror under the lid, a cheap and nasty gewgaw.

"Pannechon! Pitch that out too."

Sleep now. No, not yet! Just one more find—a tin of metal polish. Happily it is the last. I draw my greatcoat well up over my eyes and stretch myself out luxuriously. It is warm, it is good, and there is nothing at all to grumble at. Until tomorrow, and then the Boches!

Monday, September 14th. It is raining, of course. The march beneath this sad and watery sky is going to be a detestable one. I resign myself in advance to a day of saturation.

Resignation indeed is difficult of attainment when one knows, as we do, the increase of our sufferings the rain involves: the heavy clothes the coldness which penetrates with the water; the hardened leather of our boots; trousers flapping against the legs and hindering each stride; the linen at the bottom of the knapsack—that precious linen, the feel of which against one's skin is a sheer delight—hopelessly stained, transformed little by little into a sodden mass on which papers and bottles of pickles have left their stain; the mud that spurts into one's face and covers one's hands; the confused arrival; the night all too short for sleep passed beneath a coat that freezes instead of warming; the whole body stiff, joints without suppleness, painful; and the departure with boots of wood which crush the feet like the torture-shoe. Hard, indeed, is resignation!

As yesterday we march between two lines of French corpses. They seem to be dressed in new clothes, so much rain has fallen on them. It is perhaps a week since they fell. Their flesh, swollen by decomposition, has attained enormous dimensions; they have legs and arms of tremendous size, yet curiously short, and their clothes are stretched to bursting over their inflated bodies. Men of line regiments, then Colonials. The dead we passed previously were lying face downward;

these have been raised and propped against the slope facing the road, as though to watch us pass. Their faces are blackened, their lips large and swollen. Many of our men, taking them to be negroes, exclaim: "Hullo! These are Turcos."

I have a particularly vivid recollection of one of those poor dead by the roadside. He was a captain of the Colonials. They had made him kneel on the grass by forcibly bending his legs beneath him; one of his legs had gradually bent back and was stretched out in front of him, giving one the impression that the man was about to throw himself forward, as if in some erratic dance. His body was turned sideways, but his head craned rigidly forward, and his eyes were fixed on the road in a vacant stare. But what struck me most was his moustache, light and curly and altogether charming. Beneath it the mouth was no more than two purple pads of flesh. That fair ladies'-love moustache on a putrefying face was a heartrending spectacle.

Come! Head erect and fists clenched! No more of that weakness that a moment ago assailed me. We must look unmoved on these poor dead and seek from them the inspiration of hate. It was the Boche in his flight who dragged these sorry things to the side of the road, who arranged this horrid spectacle for our express benefit, and we must never rest until the brute has drunk our cup of vengeance to the dregs.

Impotent and childish is the fury that only inspires us with rage and the passion for vengeance instead of fear, as our foe hopes and believes.

Besides, every step forward now presents us with eloquent testimony of the completeness of the defeat they have suffered—helmets torn and pierced by our bullets, crushed and shattered by our shells; rusty bayonets; broken cartridge-belts, still full. To the left of the road in the fields are some overturned ammunition wagons and gun-carriages in pieces, the horses lying dead in a heap. In the ditch is the carriage of a shattered machine-gun; one can see the hole made by the shell—a 75. What a state the gun on that carriage must have been in! And the machine-gunners? At the bottom of the hole! Ammunition belts of coarse white canvas lie coiled in puddles.

We pick up some boots full of rain-water. I wonder whether the men from whom we took them walked barefooted through the mud merely for pleasure? In another hole we find the men themselves. Further on again we encounter crosses bearing German inscriptions. Here then are the Ottos, the Friedrichs, the Karls, and the Hermans!

Each cross bears four, five and even six names. The Germans were in a hurry; they buried their men in bunches.

A cross higher than the others attracts and holds our attention; it bears no more than three words deeply carved in big capitals:

ZWEI DEUTSCHE KRIEGER.

Is there still another challenge hidden behind this? If so, it is obscure. For who killed you, you two German soldiers?

Over the trampled roadway, newspapers, postcards and letters flutter. I pick up a photograph on the back of which a woman has written a few lines:

"My Peter, it is a long time since we received any news from you and we are naturally very anxious. I think, however, that very shortly you will be able to tell us of still further victories and that you will return in glory to Toelz. What a *fête* you shall have then. . . ." And then further on: "The little one has grown and is becoming quite strong. You could never imagine what a little treasure he is. Do not be too long in returning, or he will not be able to recognize you."

Sad enough, indeed, is it not? Whose, however, is the fault? Remember our dead of a short while ago; remember the captain flung almost across the road. What has he done, of what is he capable, this Peter, this German whose photograph shows him with lowered face, cold eyes, heavy-jawed, resting his hand on the back of a chair on which his wife is seated, smiling but negligible? Pity at such a moment would shame us. Let us harden our hearts and keep them hard until the end comes.

Saint-André. On a hillock just beyond the village we come upon the remains of a dressing-station. The site is marked by a fine confusion. Red-haired cowhide cases scattered about, all yawning and emptied of their contents; bayonets in their black sheaths; severed cartridge-belts; helmets without their spikes; linen torn and stained with mud and blood; packages of dressings by the hundred; pieces of cotton wool saturated by the rain lying in the middle of tiny blood-stained pools. The great trees rising above the hillock seem to be contemplating this sad chaos, while the rain drips from their branches softly and unceasingly.

We pass before Souilly. A windmill for raising water spreads its giant sails fanwise over a huge grey metal armature. Some silent houses which have escaped the shells: the melancholy of deserted houses which is almost as poignant as the sadness that clings to ruins.

A halt under the rain and quarters at Sivry-la-Perche, in a barn with green doors like all those on the Meuse. Rifles are piled on the threshing-floor, knapsacks hung on the pegs. The granary dominates the neighbourhood and is full of hay and straw. So lofty is it, that the walls become lost to sight in the darkness before meeting the rafters.

September 15th-17th.

Yet one more long march, this time straight across the entrenched camp of Verdun. Thierville is our nearest point to the citadel. Beneath a rainy sky, crossed by light clouds, lies Verdun, marked by its barracks with their roofs of coloured tiles, and the aviation field with its white hangars, and the towers of its cathedral rising high above trees and houses.

All the surrounding villages are alive with troops. Many questions are flung about as we pass through. Many of the men rush to the public fountains whose water flows into a stone basin, swallow a quart or so in long gulps, and fill their flasks. The weight of my own flask at my belt gives me a sense of comfort—it is a German flask which Pannechon brought me yesterday, and which I have duly appropriated.

The Meuse. Cattle in the meadows. Then Bras and afterwards Vacherauville.

Three weeks only have elapsed since I passed along this self-same road. Is it credible? It is a fact, nevertheless, although I find it difficult to convince myself of the reality of it. For what have I not experienced in the way of new and intense sensations, what a richness of impressions I have acquired, what dangers run? How altogether undreamed of has that life been! Confusion about me and within me; then habit swiftly succeeding the chaos of the early days. Three weeks only since I passed along this road, a very raw recruit, and now here am I a seasoned soldier.

We rested the night at Louvemont, a dirtier village than all the dirty villages we have come across so far. We are able to obtain milk, white cheese and a few small pots of honey. These things at least aid us to digest the anathemas

Captain C—— has showered upon us since our arrival, because we have dared openly to display one or two signs of weariness.

We spend a doubtful, uncertain day at Louvemont. Some heavy batteries behind the village keep firing at regular intervals, sending their heavy shells whizzing high above our heads. The Germans do not reply.

For several hours we were in the fields—no one knew why—engaged in apparently aimless manoeuvres in open formation as if under curtain-fire. Did a cautious prudence dictate this course, or were our actions consequent upon certain information received? One thing at least is certain, and that is that in the evening, shortly after we had returned to the village, a dozen or so 'crumps' were sent over to us. One of them struck a house on the opposite side of the road at the moment we were sitting down to dinner. It smashed the roof—one could hear that distinctly—passed into the house, smashed a chair on which the regimental doctor had placed his tunic, and finally embedded itself in the wall without exploding. The doctor was not in the house at the time; but when he returned it was to find the copper fuse of a large 150 directly pointing towards his bed. He went out and sought more comfortable quarters.

We left the village this morning. In the first place we took up a position in line of sections of four among some stunted acacias covering the side of a stony ravine.

I was seated near Porchon, so exhausted and weary that from time to time I sank involuntarily against his shoulder. My brain seemed to have become pap, and my inability to think caused me almost physical pain. A single tenacious impression remained in my mind—the pursuit was ended; somewhere near here the Boches had turned, and now I must fight once more, notwithstanding this breakdown of body and mind. I felt most miserably lonely, which loneliness brought in its train a black despair I simply could not resist. Not a letter had I received from my people since the day I first set out, not a word of affection, nothing, nothing at all. And they, too, what could they know of me? Had they received the cards, scribbled in haste between the bombardments, or at the side of the road during a halt, or written in the evening in the barn, by the light of a flickering candle? They did not know in what part of the world to look for me. I had been in the battle, but they remained completely ignorant as to what had occurred to me in that battle. Anxiety would have racked them throughout these long and interminable days; and I, who would prefer death a thousand times to complete solitude, was deprived of their affectionate news so essential to my well-being.

That evening we were told off for outpost duty at the edge of a wood, and before me lay two atrocious days of suffering and discouragement; two days the memory of which I hope will fortify me against any future trials, seeing that I had sufficient strength on that occasion to hold on and not disgrace myself.

Saturday, September 19th. Forty hours we pass in a ditch full of water. The improvised roof of branches and straw soon lets all the rain through. Since then we live in the midst of a torrent.

Motionless, and packed tight together in cramped and painful attitudes, we shiver in silence. Our sodden clothes freeze our skin; our saturated caps bear down on our temples with slow and painful pressure. We raise our feet as high as we can before us, but often it occurs that our frozen fingers give way, letting our feet slip down into the muddy torrent rushing along the bottom of the trench. Already our knapsacks have slipped into the water, while the tails of our greatcoats trail in it.

The slightest movement causes pain. I couldn't get up if I wanted to. A short while ago the adjutant attempted to do so; the effort wrung a cry from him, so keen were the pains in his knees and back; and then he sank down on top of us before slipping back into the hole in the mud his body had made, and resuming his former huddled attitude, which had caused his ankles to stiffen.

Nowadays I find it difficult to recall all that befell in the course of those two days; memory is veiled and dim. It is as though I had lived in an atmosphere of numbness in which all light and beauty were but dead things. An intense pain about my heart, never moving, rendered me almost delirious.

I remember that we remained for a long time hidden in a large thicket. My section was stationed near the battalion horses, which had been picketed together. Every time they moved, branches broke and fell. And most certainly it was raining, there could be no doubt of that; for long afterwards the eternal pitter-patter of rain on the leaves remained in my ears. Afterwards, I do not know how long, we set out on the march.

Almost insensibly a depressing evening settled down over fields and woods. Before us were extended the columns of infantry, clinging like ants on the side of the bare slope. Above us, the smoke balls of shrapnel, soft and pale, hung in the air. This shrapnel gave no warning of its approach, and shells burst with an abrupt snap which found no echo over the dull countryside. A deserted farm to the left had been stripped of its reddish tiles, which lay smashed to pieces on the earth. A horseman was moving slowly towards this farm, his head covered by the hood of his cloak; his horse seemed merely to glide onwards, strangely silent. The stillness was portentous, almost tangible.

We passed a night in another trench in reserve, where we are at present. Five or six of us in a bunch hung over a few damp pieces of wood we had collected in the hope of being able to make a fire; the sticks smoked but refused to burst into flame. I recollect that I was obsessed by a feverish and loquacious gaiety; I scorned my own sad condition and laboured tremendously to prevent myself giving way to the fever running riot in my veins. This lasted some time, and so nervous was I, so disordered was my speech, that those about me watched me queerly and significantly. The moment came when my ill-timed jests became an insult to the general depression. I fell silent then, and resignedly delivered myself up to that dumb despair which had been dogging my heels for days, waiting only the opportunity to enter into its kingdom.

The monotonous, incessant tapping of the rain on the leaves of the trees was in itself maddening. The sticks in the brazier hissed and spluttered. There was a single spark, a faint glow among the cinders, which I watched desperately.

In the morning firing was heard in the direction of the outposts. The captain sent me with two sections to reinforce them. We marched in single file, slipping on the greasy clay, falling every few steps; laboriously climbing on hands and knees a little ascent which, but for the mud, I could have taken in a couple of strides.

Arriving at our destination, we were compelled to seek shelter behind the trunks of trees, for all along the edge of the wood bullets were whistling. There were no trenches and the men were lining a ditch, standing in the water with their knap- sacks before them.

The rain did not cease. It flooded the vast ploughed lands, where here and there groups of walnut trees seemed to huddle shiveringly together. Two German *vedettes* posted before a wood facing ours seemed like two stone statues. Shortly afterwards infantry emerged from the wood and advanced over open ground, as dark as the soil itself, and scarcely visible. We killed several of them and they went back hastily, abandoning their dead.

Still the bullets continued to whistle. From time to time a cry burst from one of the men in the ditch, and he would come into the wood towards us, both hands pressed against his chest or staring at the blood dripping from his fingertips with wide, terrified eyes. At last the firing ceased and calmness reigned.

We returned into reserve, carrying one of my corporals who was wounded in the groin by a bullet that had passed right through it.

That was a difficult journey over the muddy roads! The wounded man groaned feebly, his arms passed around the necks of two of his comrades, his head swaying, his face livid. Once the men carrying him slipped and fell to their knees, and the agonized cry which broke from the sufferer echoed in my ears long after it had died to silence.

The night was like the preceding one; a silent, palpitating wait, the minutes as long drawn as hours; incessantly yearning for the dawn which never appeared. I grew gradually drowsy, and at length fell asleep in a heap on a comrade. He violently thrust me off, swearing savagely; I did my best to express my resentment. A little later, sudden anguish caused me to jump to my feet. I had upset the brazier, by this time almost extinct, and I had placed my hand on a few still glowing fragments of wood.

The rain continues to fall.

It is daylight now. We have just eaten a morsel or two of cold meat, wet and stale, as well as a few green potatoes found in one of the fields and partially cooked in patches beneath the cinders. We have been promised relief in the evening, but I am in such a condition now that I hope for nothing. Things have become very vague and ill-defined. I imagine that we must have been where we are at present for a very, very long time. We have been sent here; we have been commanded to remain here; and we have been forgotten. It is quite simple. No one will come. No one could come to replace us at the edge of this wood, in this ditch, beneath this rain.

Never again shall we see snug houses with a bright fire in the grate, or well-built barns filled with hay which never gets wet. Never again shall we undress to stretch our cramped limbs and rid them of this terrible iciness. And what good would it be if we could? My clothes, stiff with mud, the *puttees* crushing my legs, my hardened boots, the straps of my equipment, have not all these things become part of me and of my sufferings? They are me! The water which first saturated my skin runs now in my very veins. What am I indeed but a muddied mass swamped with water, cold to the very heart, cold as the straw which, covers us, cold as the trees on which each leaf rustles and shivers, cold as the very earth of the fields, which little by little is dissolving beneath the flooding rains?

Yesterday perhaps there was still time. Then we could have regained grip of ourselves, compelled our wills to resist. But today the evil has gone too far, has progressed beyond all hope of reparation. It is too late. It is not even worth the trouble of hoping for. . . .

Sunday, September 20th.

"By the way, old man, when will you have finished with the whole of the blanket?"

Since we got into bed that is the third time Porchon has passed that same remark. I ignore him, most properly, striving hard to make my feigned snores sound regular and natural.

"Here, you blockhead, here! When the deuce will you stop bagging all the blanket?"

The beast persists! He is asking for it and gets it!

"Dry up—you're a nuisance! Take your beastly blanket, roll yourself in it, swelter in it, take it all for yourself, only leave me alone to sleep in peace!"

Porchon contrives to remain silent for at least a minute; then, in a sleepy voice:

"I say!"

"Well, what is it now?"

"It is a bit better here than in the Haumont Wood, what?"

"Rather!"

"Better even than the barn at Louvemont, don't you think?"

"Naturally! . . . But say, old man, don't you think we had better go to sleep?"

Two minutes later and Porchon is snoring. But no longer is there sleep for me. Scenes and memories have been evoked and flit across my mind to keep me constantly wakeful. What devil of mischief prompted the idiot to mention those things? He has set the machine working and now there is no stopping it!

And so in memory I live again through bad days, nightmare days— the *réveil* in the furious, stinging rain; the arrival at Louvemont, that indescribable village little better than a sewer. I had gone over to the quarters of the adjoining section because before their barn a little chimney-piece had been erected with some paving stones. There had been a fire of flaming logs, hissing and spluttering. We had stripped ourselves to the waist to let the grateful warmth of the flames play on our chests and backs and shoulders. Sitting on a bundle of straw we had found an old, white-bearded soldier, dreaming. I had gone up to him and said:

"Hallo, M——! So you are better! Beginning to feel alive once again, eh?"

"Oh, yes, Lieutenant. But it has been a hard pull, a very hard pull! . . .''

95

And he had repeated in a low voice, as though experiencing again hardships still recent: "Very hard!"

Poor old man! He had gone through the campaign of '70 as a volunteer, and since those days had lived outside France. For thirty years, I believe, he acted as a notary in California, until the very day, in fact, which had brought this war upon us. Then, when France was once more attacked and menaced, he had flung everything aside and had come back to shoulder his rifle. He had described himself as being robust, smart and well able to endure any hardships. They had accepted his statement and sent him up to face the Boches with the first batch of reinforcements. He had joined up with us in the woods at the very moment we were setting out for those nightmarish advance posts; those two terrible succeeding days were the first of his service. Poor old man!—and he was sixty-four years of age!

The following night Pannechon had made me up a deep and fragrant bed of hay, just before I set out for mess. Dinner ended, I returned to the barn, humming softly to myself, and enjoying in anticipation a night of warmth and slumber. I entered the barn and stumbled in the dark. Good, here's the ladder! . . . One, two, three steps—the bed should be here! Groping about, I felt my revolver case and linen bag; then my hands encountered not the hay bed, soft and rounded, but a firm, extended and rather rough surface. What in the name of the mysteries could this be? A voice, muffled by the hay, enlightened me with disconcerting abruptness:

"Eh, my friend! when you have quite finished exploring my back, perhaps you will tell me what it is you want!"

One of my *poilus* had found the bed so inviting that he had appropriated it. Of course, when he discovered my identity, he flooded me with fantastic excuses. However, we spread the bed out a little and slept soundly beside each other for eight hours on end.

That morning we had moved on a short distance, *via* Douaumont, Fleury, Eix, across a countryside covered either with mud or trees, dominated by the forts with their grass-grown glacis and cupolas. We had crossed the line from Verdun to Conflans, marching ankle-deep in wet coal-dust. Before a smoke-blackened house at the barrier some enormous *girasols* thrust forth their yellow and black *corollae*, their colours rendered more brilliant by the recent rain. We passed some squads of territorials with their tools on their shoulders, artillerymen from the big fortresses, slow-moving country wagons laden with forage, tree-trunks and wine casks. Wooden huts had been erected along the roadside, each of which had a name inscribed on it, such as: Happy Villa; The Good Children's Castle; Villa Piccolo, etc. Verses adorned some of them, not of high poetical attainment, but something after this fashion:

You never see us weeping here—
Often you'll see us drinking beer.
War may not be the best of fun,
But we'll stick it till we've smashed the Hun!

Some of these cabins were constructed of logs and roofed with pine branches, the most thickly-tufted ones, of course. The points of the spikes were turned downwards to prevent the rain trickling through to the layer of thatch below. The huts, erected at the owners' caprice, were much scattered, and followed the meanderings of the rising ground to the summit of a slight elevation dominating the road to the right.

The doors, wide opened and yawning, revealed a dark, mysterious space, and made it appear almost as if the side of the slope was riddled with fathomless holes, while the bundles of brushwood made irregular green blots, clear and bright in the neighbourhood of the roadway, growing darker and vaguer as they approached the elevation, finally to vanish completely amid the undergrowth.

At length we arrived at Moulinville, where the quartermaster discovered an empty house, not yet too filthy for habitation, because the owner of it, on mobilization, had been stationed close at hand, and came over from time to time. Indeed, he turned up while we were dining—a huge "Meusien," with a high colour, stiff, cropped hair and looking gigantic in his artilleryman's cloak. He personally conducted us to a room, the floor of which creaked, and pointing to a bed informed us with tremendous pride and dignity that:

"You are welcome to sleep there, if you wish, but I shall not be able to supply you with sheets."

Sheets! And he was quite crestfallen, this good-hearted artilleryman, because he could not give us any sheets! We, Porchon and myself, certainly did not waste many regrets on such things when we climbed into bed a few moments ago and drew the curtains! Does the absence of sheets worry him, this hearty snorer at my side, perspiring as he is between the ticking and an eiderdown? It is certainly warm—perhaps even a little too warm. I am hot all over, back and front. From head to foot am I wet. It is as if I were sleeping in a bath!

Monday, September 21st.

The cyclist of our company awakens me by shouting in my ear: "Do you not wish to breakfast, Lieutenant?"

He is carrying two bowls of black coffee, with two slices of golden-brown toast, most appetizing to look upon.

The hothouse kind of night we have passed has, I find, robbed me of all force and energy. My body is languid, my tongue thick, my scalp irritates. And as for Porchon, he cannot even open his eyes. He wrinkles up his face; a tremendous effort and the lids part; but they are so heavy that they close again.

Everything is slack today and rather depressing because of that slackness. I wandered slowly through the muddy streets. What am I going to do? In a couple of hours' time we are going to dine. That at least will be something, but what to do until that time?

I go from door to door on a commandeering expedition—a fowl, jam, wine, "it doesn't matter what, anything you have." Small success attends my effort. I obtain only a few onions and a bottle of liqueur, weak and oversweetened, obtained only after a struggle and at a preposterous price.

The adjutant whom I meet offers me a drink.

A quarter of an hour afterwards Major C—— calls for me and asks me to call at the house where he is messing with the ensign. Waiters are opening bottles of preserves, and carving meat. The major bursts in on them:

"Look sharp! Fetch a cloth, three glasses, and 'the' bottle and some water."

One more drink! Well, I suppose so, but my heaviness increases. I go back to my room, where I find a sleepy Porchon stretched out in a chair looking vaguely into space.

"What are we going to do? Shall we play *écarté?*"

He unfolds a piece of newspaper and takes out a pack of greasy cards. We sit down to play:

"The king! . . . Pass . . . trump . . . trump. . . ."

"Ah, *zut!* What can you do with a game like this?"

"Again the king . . . trump. . . ."

But I fear I am not in a sociable mood. Porchon suddenly throws down his cards and says:

"I play no longer. I have had enough. You worry me. . . . And, after all, I bore myself. I think we had better go to bed early this evening!"

I am also bored with myself and think only of bed. A night such as last night, after all our trials, is either not enough or too much. Just one more, or more than one, and we shall have regained all our strength and spirits. Let us be thankful for small mercies. Of tonight at least we are certain, and although we do not know it, it may be that others are to follow. We have been informed we may anticipate a few days' rest in billets on the left bank of the Meuse.

Five o'clock in the evening. An order is circulated:

It is probable that the ——th Infantry Division will move on tonight. Distribute the rations at once and be ready to leave at any moment.

So much for our night's rest! It appears that a reserve division has been thrown into confusion near the Spada Gap. We must go up in support. Gone is all hope of the night's rest, anticipated and almost promised us !. . . Still, one more effort to accept events with resignation, to obey implicitly any and all orders given us, no matter what they may be; once more the contortion which hoists the pack on to the back, an ever-present burden.

We leave at eight o'clock, with a long march through the night before us. The villages of Chatillon-sous-les-Côtes, Watronville, Ronvaux are passed. They are all full of soldiers, the murmur of whose voices comes to us through the darkness. Moonlight struggles feebly through the chinks of the old doors of barns; clear fires are burning before the houses and gleaming on ammunition dumps, over which men are squatting and keeping guard.

"Where are we?" ask some of our men. "At Paname," voices reply. "In the Meuse!"

"If anyone asks you, say you know nothing." These and other answers we receive. Haudiomont once again. The night is advancing; kitchen fires are going out now, but from time to time the wind sends a tiny flame leaping out of a brazier which flickers and dies to darkness again.

We enter the forest of Amblonville, black and immense.

The faintly-marked path winds ahead until lost to view between trees which overhang it to right and left, and seem to be marching up as though to descend upon us and crush us. I experience a sense of oppression. At first we marched towards the south-west, then towards the south-east; now we are again marching towards the south-west. And three hours have passed since first we plunged into the wood. I feel as if I were sinking into mud which becomes thicker and thicker

99

each moment. When may we hope to reach the bottom?

At last the sky can be seen between the trees, and the darkness lightens little by little. Now I begin to breathe more freely. The moon has disappeared; but the sky is thick with innumerable stars. A sentinel at a crossroad stamps his feet to keep them warm. We question him:

"Are there any Boches about here?"

"I think so," he replied. "There is a good chance of coming across them tomorrow."

"Where are they?"

"Towards Amblonville farm."

"Is it far from here?"

"Near Mouilly, two, three miles; you have your back to it."

"And then! . . . (*Censored*)! . . .

. . . (*Censored*)!..."

The men begin to hum.

". . . . (*Censored*)! . . ."

"Silence behind there!" I bawl out. "Aubert, Lardin, silence! you fools! Or that little lullaby of yours won't have a pleasant ending!"

An abrupt halt, marking time.

Here we are, at Rupt-en-Wöevre. The regiment bivouacs in a field at one end of the village. I know nothing at all of the situation, and I find it difficult to take my bearings. The hour is now two in the morning.

We are chilled to the marrow. Porchon and I sit down, back to back, tapping one foot against the other while awaiting the coming of the day. The cold steals up our legs and stiffens them. We find it quite impossible to maintain our position. I tramp up and down a sloping road before some barns. From time to time a man half opens one of the doors and creeps in. By Jove! That's a good idea! I steal into one of the barns to find some thirty men already in occupation. An hour passes, maybe two, during which I sit half on a sack, half on an old hen, who ruffles herself and grumbles constantly.

Dawn cold and stark. We light a fire and endeavour to restore our circulation.

6

In the Woods

Tuesday, September 22nd. I start a few letters, fingers frozen, nose wet:

"I do not know how I look; but to tell the truth, my powers of resistance have astonished even myself. It is strange and marvellous how everyone among us appears to possess a faculty for adapting himself to the immediate circumstances. Our hard life has hardened us and will keep us so, for however long it may continue. At the present moment, it would seem as if we had been born to wage war, to sleep in the open no matter what the weather, to eat when, where, and what we can, also as much as we can. You have a cloth on your table? Spoons, forks, all kinds of forks—for the oysters, the fruits, the snails, and so on? You even have a clean plate for each course—isn't it funny? Glasses are placed before you of all shapes and sizes, so fragile that a pressure of the hand would break them. And you drink your coffee—I have a vague memory that this is so—out of a fine glass which is not the same as that from which you drink your tea, for example! But how complicated all that is! We others have our pocket-knife, our mugs, and our fingers! I assure you they are quite sufficient. . . ."

An interruption. A woman appears, thin and dirty, pushing before her a little yellow-haired girl, whose eyes are red-rimmed and tear-stained. The doctor having been consulted, prescribes for colic.

"And what do I owe you for that, doctor?" asks the woman.

"Nothing at all, madam."

But she draws from beneath her apron a dusty bottle. "I must 'recompinse' you somehow. There is not very much in it, but what there is tastes good. It is good: oh, but indeed it is!"

It is Toul wine, dry, thin and somewhat sharp. A brawn, turned out on to a plate, gives us an excellent lunch.

In the afternoon we pass to the observation trench. We overtake a group of lame men, without weapons, coats open, almost all of them limping along with a stick. Among them I recognize a friend of pre-war days. We shake hands and speak eagerly and with pleasure of common memories, before approaching the inevitable regrets. As he belonged to a regiment which was compelled to give way before the Boches, I asked him how it had come about. He shrugged his shoulders despondently.

"Masses of infantry; an endless hail of shell; not a gun to support us . . . don't let's talk about it, old man."

After the iciness of the preceding night, a day of burning sunshine. I am wearing ridiculously thin boots, which decrease in size as my feet swell. I give stones a wide berth.

To the right of the road the fields roll away like a great cloth, fresh and green until they reach the heights covered with trees, whose luxuriant foliage seems to fall from the top to the bottom of the slopes.

"Single file through the cutting."

That is the sign that we are entering the zone of fire of the German guns. We climb and pass through the village of Mouilly, built on the side of a slope. Almost all the houses, with their plaster *façades*, are on one side of the road, the left. On the other side meadows stretch away to where the sun rises and where the green of the wooded highlands begins its cascade to the plains below. Enormous shell-holes mark the meadows, about which the upflung earth forms brown circles which look from the distance like enormous stains.

Woods. Some shrapnel bursts ahead of us, but far away. In the cutting we encounter a big grey motorcar, ornamented with gilt letters. One of its wheels has been blown away and its steel sides bear the mark of shells: it was the product of some great Leipzig firm.

We overtake a regiment of the division at the end of the wood on the Mouilly-Saint-Rémy road. A fight has taken place, and our 75's are still sending down a rain of shells, forming a barrage some five hundred yards before us. We stand and watch it, Porchon and I, together with the two officers we are going to relieve. They are both fine soldiers and speak unaffectedly of the battle they have just passed through. One of them, tall, bony, with tanned skin and black eyes almost feverishly keen above a fine nose, expresses himself shortly and precisely. The second, small, rather too affable, with a wrinkled face, laughing eyes, fresh lips and a brown beard, entertains us with a recital of horrors in a cheerful voice and warns us that we are very likely to "leave our skins over there."

The thunder of the 75's almost splits our ears. Occasionally a German shell flies past us with a shrill whistle and peppers the trees with a volley of shrapnel. Into the midst of this tumult we march and take up position. My section occupies about fifty yards of a trench already full of corpses.

"Out with your tools," I say to my men, "and dig for all you are worth."

Night falls. The cold increases. It is that hour when, the battle ended, the wounded who have not yet been brought in, cry aloud in their suffering and distress. And those calls, those appealings, those moanings, awaken anguish in all those compelled to listen to them; an anguish the crueller for the fighters who are chained to their posts by stern duty yet who long to rush out to their gasping comrades, to dress their wounds, to speak words of comfort to them, and to carry them to safety where fires burn brightly and warm. Yet we must not do so; we are chained to the spot, our hearts wrung, our nerves quivering, shivering at the sound of soul-stricken cries brought to us unceasingly by the night.

"A drink! . . ."

"Are you going to leave me to die here? . . ."

"Stretcher-bearers! . . ."

"Drink! . . ."

"Ah! . . ."

"Stretcher-bearers! . . ."

I hear some of my men say:

"Where the devil are the stretcher-bearers!"

. . . (*Censored.*) . . .

"They are like fleas—you can never find them when you look for them."

And before us the whole plain wrapped in darkness seems to shiver from the agony of those undressed wounds.

Voices soft, weary from having cried so long:

". . . (*Censored.*) . . .

"Mother, oh, mother!"

"Jeanne, little Jeanne. . . . Oh! say that you hear me, my Jeanne!"

"I am thirsty. . . . I am thirsty. . . . I am thirsty. . . . I am thirsty. . . ."

Voices in anguish, panting and gasping:

"I won't die here like a rat!"

"Stretcher-bearers! Stretcher-bearers! ... Stretcher-bearers!!!"

"... (*Censored.*) ...

......?"

"You fellows, finish me off, for God's sake! Ah! ..."

A German, not more than twenty yards away, cries out incessantly:

"*Kamerad! Franzose! Kamerad! Kamerad! Franzose!*"

And in a lower voice:

"*Hilfe! Hilfe!*"

His voice wavers and breaks into a wailing as of a crying child; then his teeth snap fiercely; then he shatters the night stillness with a beast's cry, like the howling of a dog baying at the moon.

Terrible beyond the power of words, that night. Every minute either Porchon or myself were jumping to our feet. The whole time we were under fire and the cold was truly cursed.

Wednesday, September 23rd,

Relief appears at last. We depart through the woods along a pathway from which the undergrowth has been cleared, thus permitting us to see well ahead. During a short halt, several of the men break into exclamations of pleasure and delight:

"Hallo! Vauthier!"

"And you, Raynaud!"

"Well, I'm damned. ... Baurain!"

"It is not possible! We thought you had gone for good. ... What have you been doing? ... Where do you come from?"

Three men report to me and show that they were ordered to rejoin on this date. I am pleased, for the three men, intelligent, devoted, and brave, are among the best under my command.

(*Suppressed by the Censor.*)

In going towards Mouilly, we repass the big grey motorcar at the side of the road. A little further on, the ranks open a little without command, in order not to disturb a wounded horse. It is a magnificent, black beast, a king of its kind. Shrapnel has wounded it in the chest and broken one of its shoulders, from which the blood streams right down to the hoof to form a pool in the dust. Its flanks are quivering with the agony it is enduring, while the shattered leg is violently trembling. The sufferings of this poor, gasping, dumb brute, dying minute by minute, and the pathetic, pain-darkened eyes with which it watches us as we pass, stir every man among us as if we were looking upon human agony. . . .

The nearer we approach the village, the more numerous become the wounded men returning from the fight. They come in groups, carefully selecting the shorter grass to walk over, seeking the shade to avoid the burning sun, which makes their wounds smart intolerably. There are a few Germans mingled with our men; one big-built man, fair, ruddy and with blue eyes, is assisting a little French infantryman, who limps along jesting and laughing and displaying all his teeth. With a wicked glance towards us, he cries aloud to the Boche:

"Is it not true, you pig, that you are a good pig?"

"I understand," exclaims the German gutturally. "Pig, good pig! I understand!"

And an unctuous laugh spreads all over his greasy face, happy at this display of camaraderie which promises so well for him, as vile and loathsome as are all Boches when at the mercy of a conqueror.

Mouilly. Other roads descend from the woods, all choked with processions of wounded, and still more wounded, moving slowly down into the village. Dressing-stations have been set up in the barns; about them is a litter, constantly increasing, of stained bandages and blood-soaked pieces of cotton-wool, extending in some cases almost into the middle of the road. From the interior of the barns emanate sharp cries, speaking eloquently of bitter pain and endurance; the air reeks with the pungent smell of iodoform.

About the little church, with its shell-shattered windows, lies the cemetery, with its mossy tombstones and rust-eaten metal crosses. Empty, newly-dug graves yawn; so many little mounds bear the fresh marks of the pick! And towards this cemetery some stretcher-bearers come, walking slowly and in time, carrying between them stretchers, hurdles, stepladders, on which still figures lie, rigid beneath the rough cloth covering them.

We come to a halt near the Amblonville Farm, whose spacious and strongly-built walls look down over wide and rolling grass-lands, moist and verdant. The Mouilly Road terminates there: it stretches away before us, crossing a stream over a little stone bridge, passes a silver-surfaced lake, which acts as a mirror to the superb trees about it, to become winding and narrow near some sombre woods, amid which a half-hidden windmill arises, and finally scales the abrupt heights behind which lies the village.

Behind the summit some 75's are firing steadily and slowly. Lower down, guns, horses and their drivers, and ammunition wagons, appearing as though sighted through the wrong end of a telescope, flow almost imperceptibly this way and that, like weeds slowly waving in the depths of a river.

We make a fire, and soon potatoes begin to glaze and blacken among the glowing cinders. As a matter of sheer habit we eat them, defying such inconveniences as dyspepsia or enteritis or dysentery, from one or the other of which almost all of us have suffered for a month past.

German aeroplanes come circling above us in the course of the afternoon. Our shells hurtle towards them like gigantic rockets minus their tail of sparks. Puffs of smoke, shot through for an instant by a golden glow, follow the aircraft, describing drifting circles about them, white as driven snow. They continue their flight, however, wheeling through space like birds of prey, watching always. A few bombs are dropped, burying themselves in the earth about us. One of them explodes violently, rather uncomfortably close at hand. The cyclist, who was lying down, jumped hastily to his feet and examined his foot.

"Not a scratch!" he exclaimed. "It only cut open my shoe!"

Down into the grass where he had been dozing he sank again, waving his hand towards the whistling shells:

"You up there! Let us have no more of your impertinence."

Having carefully arranged his handkerchief over his face, to shield his eyes from the sun, he continued to grumble under cover of it:

"A good pair of bath-pumps gone for nothing! I have a good mind to give up marching altogether!"

An hour later a few smoke-wreathed whizz-bangs pass over the top of the hill and fall alongside our batteries. One or two burst directly above the medley of traffic in the roadway, causing the microscopical horses (as they appeared to us), to rear and kick, and sending men, who looked to be no more than big insects, running this way and that; finally the whole concourse, like a long-drawn ribbon, moves away to vanish beneath the trees to the left. The guns remain in position.

The sunset this evening over the valley is limpid and indescribably beautiful. The sky pales to the zenith as the sinking sun glides from transparent emerald to its bed of many golds, which deepen to the crimson of leaping flames on the skyline.

Thursday, September 24th.

One half the company is quartered at the farm. A stroke of luck enabled me to snatch a good four hours' sleep in the hay. Of course there was bound to be one fly in the amber. Our barn, big and lofty, was a veritable trap for draughts. Moreover, the noise of a continual coming and going, quarrels among the men regarding their respective berths, or a lost water-bottle, or a rifle that had been substituted for another one, created an unceasing din hardly propitious to sleep. With the dawn we march back to our meadow. Once more we wait and wait, with nothing to do, knowing nothing.

Ten o'clock! An order comes to hand: "The men must get their food now or not at all, and be ready to move at a moment's notice."

The cooks are in a very bad temper because the haricot beans, defying all efforts and coaxings, remain obdurately hard.

"Not worth while making oneself ill with such stuff! They would blow out a wooden horse! "

"Of course if the men don't mind chewing shrapnel!"

I advise my men to cook what meat they have, so that, if necessary, it can be eaten on the road as we go along.

It appears I was wise in my generation, for very shortly the "Fall in!" sounds, and we set off at once, evidently in the direction of Mouilly.

It is odd, but we cannot hear the faintest sound of fighting, not even the snap of a rifle or the boom of a gun. Yet over the hilltop there comes at a trot towards us a non-commissioned officer of mounted *chasseurs*, his head swathed in blood-stained bandages. Although rather pale, he sits erect in his saddle and smiles cheerfully.

"Hit?" someone calls out.

"Nothing to talk about. A shell splinter shaved my head."

Questions follow him along the road.

"Is it very unhealthy over there?"

"A little, my son. Just wait five minutes and you will have something to show as good as anything you will find at Mouilly!"

Down in the village Red Cross officers are fussing about. We meet two motorcars travelling at full speed and raising a suffocating cloud of dust.

Wounded men drag themselves along, without equipment or rifles, their chests bare, uniforms tattered, hair wet with perspiration, white-cheeked and bloodstained. They have improvised bandages out of their handkerchiefs, shirt-sleeves or towels. They walk stoopingly, heads bent, hunched to one side, by reason of broken shoulders or arms that hang listless and heavy. Some are crawling, some are hopping on one foot, some with the aid of two sticks drag behind them a lifeless limb, smothered in bandages. There are faces so swathed that only the eyes appear, feverish and distressed; others in which only one eye is visible, the other hidden beneath dressings through which the blood percolates and trickles down bristly chins. And here are two wounded men on stretchers, their faces waxlike and shrunken, nostrils pinched, eyes closed and shadowed, bloodless hands clutching the sides of the ambulance; behind them huge drops mark their course through the dust.

"An ambulance! Where can I find an ambulance?" ask some of the other wounded of the bearers.

"Where are you going to be sent to?"

"I say, you fellow there! Have you got any bandages?"

"Give him your flask, I say; give it to him! . . ."

Looking upon all which sights, the nerves of my men begin to suffer as I can plainly see.

" . . . (*Censored*) ....!"

Some of the wounded joke light-heartedly:

"Eh! Binet, now were you careful to number your giblets? . . ."

"Oh, my mother! If you could only see your son's face now!"

"Thank the good Boches for my nice wound; a billet at Nice, the Côte d'Azur and the Casinos where you can scratch up the gold with little rakes!"

"So you've been saving up now?"

"Saving! I should think so. Live carefully on a bullet a day, and it doesn't take you long to become a millionaire."

But gaiety finds no echo. The men fall silent, stricken with nameless forebodings. Suddenly the shells hurtle whistling over the wood.

"In single file through the cutting!"

We stumble against branches, get entangled in the brambles. The grass deadens the echo of our footsteps, which a moment before resounded along the road.

"Lie down!"

The order comes not a moment too soon, for hardly have we obeyed it when a shell bursts right on top of us. Stones are flung high in the air, and simultaneously two men behind me cry out. The detonation makes my ears tingle; a heavy, acrid odour fills the air.

"Lieutenant! That was my baptism. Just look at these two little holes!"

I turn to look into a rather pale and anxious face, which nevertheless expresses great relief. The man is a corporal, newly joined. He has unbuckled his pack to show me two bullet holes running right through the roll of it.

"You will find the bullets inside, all right," I tell him. "You had better keep them as souvenirs!"

All this while another of my men, named Gaubert, is grumbling and congratulating himself at one and the same moment. He playfully exhibits his flask, a battered, pitiful object which had just intercepted a bullet on its way to his thigh.

"Bravo, my little flask—bravo, my friend! You did not want your Gaubert to be sent down; so you took his place. What a good chap you are! . . . But what do you think your Gaubert is going to drink out of now? What do you want me to drink out of? I ask you!"

But he does not throw the useless can away; instead he places it carefully in his sack.

"I shall have to use my mess-tin—but never mind!"

Listen! I fancy I can hear the sounds of firing. It gives one the impression of being far distant; yet it should be near enough to us, rather too near, in fact. Perhaps the hill to the right is obstructing the sound! Porchon is at my side, because I am marching with the leading section.

"Do you hear?" I ask him.

"Hear what?"

"Rifle fire."

"No!"

How does he manage not to hear it? I am more certain than ever now that I am not mistaken. That sort of crackling, distant perhaps, but nevertheless continuously audible, is the battle towards which we are marching, and which is being waged away over there beyond the hilltop. Let us hasten! It is imperative we should fling ourselves immediately and without hesitation into the midst of that fight, face boldly the bullets streaming and striking. Hurry we must, for wounded men are coming down towards us, followed by others in an endless file, and it is as if merely by showing themselves with their wounds and their blood and their appearance of complete exhaustion, with their anguished faces—it is as if they said and repeated again and again to my men:

"See, there is a battle raging! See what it has done for us; just look upon us returning. And there are hundreds and hundreds more who cannot follow us; who have fallen as we did, who have striven to rise, but could not, and who are lying about everywhere in the woods, dying. There are hundreds and hundreds of others who fell dead where they stood, struck in the head, in the heart, in the stomach, who have rolled over on to the moss, whose still warm bodies you will find lying about everywhere in the woods. You can see them for yourselves if you go there. But if you do go, the bullets will kill you also, as they killed them; or they will wound you, as they have wounded us. Do not go on!"

And the living flesh, shrinking instinctively from death, recoils.

"Porchon, watch the men!"

I have carefully lowered my voice and he, replying to me, does the same.

"Things look bad: I am afraid we may have trouble in a bit."

In one backward glance he has seen the faces of the men, anxious, lined with dread, distorted by nervous grimaces, every man in the grip of a tempest of fear, wide-eyed and feverish.

Still, without faltering, they march behind us. Each step forward they take brings them nearer that corner of the earth where death reigns today, yet still they march onwards. Each one with his living flesh is about to enter an inferno; yet the terror-stricken body will act as it should, will perform all the actions of a man fighting a battle. The eyes will aim and judge; the finger on the trigger will not fail. And so they will go on for as long as may be necessary, despite the bullets flying about them, whistling and singing without pause, often striking with a queer dead noise which makes one turn one's head quickly, and which seems to say: "Here! Look!" They look and see a comrade fall, and say to themselves: "In a little while perhaps it will be my turn; in an hour or a minute or even in this passing second, it will be my turn." And then every particle of their flesh will shrink and know fear. They will be afraid—that is as certain as it is inevitable; but being afraid, they will remain at their posts. And they will fight, compelling their bodies to obedience, because they know that that is what they should do, and because—well! because they are men.

By fours, through the wood and up the slope. I cannot overcome the forebodings aroused by the nervousness of my men. I have complete confidence in them and in myself; but, that confidence notwithstanding, something warns me instinctively of the presence of a new element, of a danger I cannot define even to myself, of—can it be panic? What an age we are in going up! My pulses are beating violently; the blood is rushing to my brain.

"Ah! . . ."

The instant we reach the top of the slope a volley, hissing, tearing and spitting, is directed at us. A common impulse causes the men to throw themselves flat to the earth.

"Up you get, *nom d'un chien!* Regnard, Lauche, all the N.C.O.'s ... (*Censored.*) ... Make them get up!"

The fire is not yet heavy. A few bullets only come seeking us, shattering the branches about us. I call out at the top of my voice:

"Let it be clearly understood! All N.C.O.'s are responsible for seeing that no man falls out. We are about to cross a copse where it is very easy to get away. You must keep a very sharp lookout."

Two men rush into the clearing where I am standing. They run so quickly that they appear to be flying from the foe. Their faces are bloody and no merciful bandage conceals the wounds which they are coming to show to my men! As they come up, the first man cries:

"Get out of the way! Make room! There are others following us!"

That man no longer possesses a nose; in place of it there is a hole which bleeds and bleeds. ...

His companion has had his lower jaw blown off. Is it credible a single bullet could effect such a shocking injury? Almost half his face is no more than a soft, hanging, crimson piece of flesh, from which blood and saliva trickle in a viscous stream. Above this horror peer out two round, blue, boyish eyes; they stare at me, eloquent with unendurable distress, in mute stupefaction. The sight shakes me to the very depths of my being, to the point of tears; then the unmeasured rage of a madman against those who caused this war, who set all this blood running, who massacre and mutilate, sweeps over me like a storm.

"Get out of the way! Get out of the way!" Another man is crying out the words now. Staggering and livid, he presses both his hands to the lower part of his abdomen to hold in his intestines, bulging in his crimson shirt. Another is desperately clutching his arm, from which large drops of blood drip constantly. A fourth suddenly stops running, kneels down before us, with his back towards the enemy, opens his clothes and deliberately withdraws from the inner side of the groin a bullet, which he carefully places in his purse.

And so endlessly they stream past us, each one with the same staring eyes, following the same stumbling and zigzag course, panting, obsessed by the thought of the hilltop behind which lies safety, burning to get out of this ravine where death whistles amid the leaves, in order to recover their nerves down there, where their wounds will be dressed, where they will be cared for, perhaps even saved.

"Your section will occupy the ditch which forms a continuation of

111

the Callone trench," Porchon tells me. "Keep a close watch over our left, the roadway and this clearing. You will be covering the battalion on this side."

I lead my men right into the heart of the inferno. I have to shout at the top of my voice to make the sergeant and corporals hear my orders. Behind us a machine-gun spits furiously, sweeping the road with a veritable stream of bullets. We are only just beyond the arc of its fire, and the incessant detonations follow each other so rapidly that all one can hear is a rending sound, as though the earth itself were gradually splitting asunder. At times the vicious sweep gets unpleasantly close, and a death-dealing swarm of lead whips and rends the air, dashing warm puffs into our faces. At the same time German bullets fly through the leaves; they embed themselves in the trunks of trees, shatter big branches, tear off smaller ones, which drift lightly and slowly down upon us; they fly over the road before the machine-gun bullets, which they seem to defy; it is almost as if a duel were being waged between these whistling demons which pass spattering, spluttering and ricocheting, spitefully hissing there before us over the road where the stones lie pulverized.

"Lie down at the bottom of the ditch. Good Lord, don't raise your head!"

Two of my men have now been wounded; one of them near me has sunk to his knees, and is gasping and vomiting blood; the other sits down with his back to a tree-trunk and begins to unlace his gaiters with trembling fingers in order to see "where it is," and "how it is."

The noise of galloping in the clearing. Are they coming this way? No! ..! ...!

"Well done, Morand! Bravo, my boy ! ...!"

(Suppressed by Censor.)

"What, the Boches? How will they explain it afterwards?"

"Ah, good! Here you are, Lieutenant. . . ."

A corporal stands beside me, cool and unperturbed. There is no such word as fear in the dictionary of this man.

"Some of the men broke and ran a few moments ago," he says, "and it is not good to think about. But I must say the occasion justified them. The Boches came up like rats, swarming everywhere. The thickets are full of them now; some of them are not more than fifty yards away. I assure you it is so, Lieutenant, and I am not short-sighted. There is not a single Frenchman between us and them, and they are there all right. . . ."

It is true enough, but all the same. . . . Their cursed bullets are covering every inch of ground round about us.

Suddenly their bugles ring out and their drums sound close at hand, very close. They are charging.

"Look, they're there," cries one of my men. "You can see them there."

At the end of the clearing two Germans are kneeling and firing.

"Rapid fire! Right into them! . . Fire!"

Lebels crack. The fumes of burnt powder drift beneath the trees. The German bugles sound louder; the noise of their drums almost drowns the fusillade. Behind us the machine-gun splutters with sufficient violence to destroy its own tripod.

"There they are! There they are! . . . "

The men have called out simultaneously and without any trace of fear in their voices. They are excited by the surrounding inferno, by the increasing smell of burning powder, by the sight of the enemy advancing in mass formation less than a hundred yards away—dense ranks of men in which our bullets create constant gaps. The intoxication of battle has seized the men; no longer is there thought of panic.

"Fix bayonets!"

"Hardly worth the trouble now. Lieutenant . . . you must retire."

A breathless voice has uttered these words, and I turn to find that Presle, my *agent de liaison*, has come up behind me. Great drops of perspiration fall from him, and he breathes pantingly, mouth wide open. One of his cartridge slings hangs severed from his belt.

"A bullet did that," he said. "Cut the sling while I was running. However, I come to inform you that you must retire behind the hill, above the Saint Remy road. We are going to hold on there. The other companies are gone already—you alone remain now. You must move quickly."

Move quickly! A very simple business, of course, considering the thorny and tangled undergrowth, which wraps itself about one's legs, binds and tears them.

"Morand, see that no one goes by the path. If they do, they'll only get cut down. They'll be mere targets. No one by the path until we meet at the top of the hill! "

It's the same old story of the poor lot who wouldn't go through the scrub at Vauxmarie. It's much easier to run by the path; there are no thorns to tear one's legs or get in the way; but certain death lurks

113

there!

"Halt! . . . Half turn . . . skirmishing formation . . . fire as you like!"

The men obey me to the letter. That is good, very good—an obedient, intelligent fighting section. My heart beats rapidly but steadily. Just now I feel sure of myself, self-possessed, happy. I want to laugh at the bullets, and I thrust my quite unnecessary revolver back into my belt.

The German bugles are now no longer sounding; their Mausers are firing only at irregular intervals. What are they up to? I determine to try and discover.

"Cease fire!"

I walk forward a few steps erect, seeking no cover. I am ready to wager that the forest is teeming with the pigs, that they will try to swamp us at twenty yards. I feel them numerous, invisible, about me. Invisible! . . . Not quite. I can see you, German beast, behind that tree, and you also to the left; your uniform is darker than the leaves. Just wait a moment, my merry men, and we'll make you a present of something. I make a signal to Morand, who has received previous instructions, and he runs up. I show him the bull's-eye.

"Just look there, behind that big ... ah! ... I have got it!"

"Lieutenant!". . . Morand's voice is startled. . . . "Are you wounded? . . . Lieutenant! . . ."

"Eh? What? . . . Oh, yes! . . ."

Some enormous projectile has caught me full in the stomach, while at the same moment a brilliant yellow streak flies before my eyes. I have fallen to my knees, doubled up, my hands pressing my stomach. How horribly painful. . . . I can no longer breathe. . . . In the stomach, too—that is serious! . . . What is going to become of my men? . . . In the stomach! If only I could see my dear ones for the last time! . . . Ah! I can breathe now. That is a bit better. Where exactly have I been struck?

I take cover behind a tree, sitting down and leaning against it. Some of the men rush towards me—I recognize them all. One of them, Delval, wants to carry me in his arms, but I find I can walk quite well alone. Even my legs do not fail me, and I can sit without any discomfort.

"No, I don't want anyone," I say. "Fall in again, I want no one."

It certainly can't be very serious. What a story it will make! In the centre of my tunic is a hole, the edges of which are frayed. I thrust my

114

finger in and draw it out again. There is just a smear of blood, nothing more. Why isn't there more?

Ah! and my belt has been cut, and the button that should be there, where has that gone? My trousers are pierced also. Here is the spot where the ball struck; a crimson patch on the skin, which is slightly torn. Just one drop of blood trickling . . . is that, then, my mortal wound?

I look stupidly at my stomach; mechanically I thrust my finger in and out of the hole in my coat . . . all at once I understand, and all my fears are instantly dissipated. Why did it take me so long to perceive what had happened?

The brilliant yellow streak that had flashed before my eyes must have been the button, now missing, struck by the bullet. For the fact that the button did not enter my body with the bullet, I must thank my belt, the surface of which is cracked where the button struck it.

But suppose the bullet had not struck the button, and my belt had not been precisely behind that button? Ah, well, my friend, these are vain speculations. In the meantime, you are acting rather grotesquely: a wounded officer who is not wounded, squatting behind a tree inspecting his stomach, while his section . . . get up, man, and back to your post!

It is surprising how slowly the Boches move. Are they too exhausted to advance? They must have lost heavily while charging up the hillside towards the summit. They are not too weary to fire, however! What a tempest! And our Lebels are speaking loudly, too, louder than ever. One can hardly hear anything in their incessant din. Only by straining the ear can one catch the spitting of the Mausers and whistling of their bullets.

Who is that up there, walking about all alone? I see it is the captain, with his eternal lance, unperturbed, eyes everywhere, quite serene. He cries out to me when he sees me:

"Hallo, is it you? I have just been told that you had a bullet in your stomach."

"So I did, Captain. But it was a harmless one this time. I am in luck."

I put myself at the head of my *poilus*. "Come along, boys! We're not going to be knocked out by that lot. Behind that pile of logs there."

There are more of our men a little further away to the right, disposed in skirmishing formation, forming an irregular but continuous line. They have made wonderfully good use of every inch of cover;

kneeling behind tree-boles or piles of logs and firing; lying down behind miniature mounds, or in holes they have dug with their picks. The terrain is splendidly utilized—these men know how to fight.

A few yards behind them their officers watch and direct their fire. One of them walks about erect, strolls from man to man, nose in the air, pipe between his teeth, hands in his pockets. With a thrill of emotion I recognize the nose, the pipe and beard as belonging to Porchon. Ah, old man, I will tell you what I think about it afterwards!

Meanwhile I place my men over to the left, thus prolonging the line. Very soon their rifles are making a chorus with those of their neighbours.

"One round! Aim! Fire!"

A few of the men are late by a second or two.

"One round! Aim! Fire!"

A single sharp explosion; no one late this time. Excellent!

"Three rounds . . . at four hundred metres . . . fire!"

The Boches are certainly not brilliant marksmen! They do not aim; their bullets either fly too high among the branches above us or fall short before us. And their bugles? And their drums? Their last charge is a feeble affair, broken, finished, dead!

"Cease fire!"

My men, hearing, pass the order along and cease fire, but keep their rifles ready, awaiting a new command.

"Two rounds. . . ."

The command runs right along the line: "Two rounds . . . two rounds . . . two rounds."

This is good! It is splendid! Only to think that a little time ago I wanted to step into the road swept by that machine-gun, in order to reassure my trembling men and avert a shameful *débâcle* which I dreaded! . . .

(*Censored.*)

Little by little the firing dies away. We ourselves fire no longer, because we have consumed an enormous amount of ammunition; the nickel cases thickly cover the ground behind the pile of logs. It must be getting late; evening falls. Lassitude descends upon the woods and us. The craving for rest becomes insistent. There are gaps in our ranks which we only know and feel when calm succeeds the storm. The moment is come when the survivors gather together and count themselves, when they regain touch with each other, when closer contact seems in some sort to deaden the sense of loss.

The order to leave the wood reaches us at the usual time; it is as though we had not been fighting at all. We have checked the rush of the Boches; we have killed hundreds of them, have decimated, dispersed and demoralized their attacking battalions. They will not advance again this evening; our day's work is done.

And slowly, silently, through the woods on which the still peace of the autumn twilight now lies, we march and so regain the Mouilly road, the misty valley, and the Amblonville farm.

In the clear, cool night, to the accompaniment of many voices, the sections assemble and line up, and the companies are reformed. How attenuated, how mutilated they look!

My poor battalion! Today's fight has once again cost us dearly. The 5th, which was so terribly cut up two weeks ago in the trenches at Vauxmarie, has also suffered cruelly again.

As for my own men, I know only too well those who are missing. Lauche, my sergeant, the only one left to me since Vauxmarie—it is always Vauxmarie!—I had seen him, as Vauthier put it, clawing the grass at the bottom of the ditch; I knew he was gone already. There was big Brunet also, and several others struck down at my side. And when I told the corporals to step forward and call out the rolls of their squads, voices responded which were not theirs. In each case a man of the "first class" or old soldier stepped forward to say:

"Corporal Regnard, wounded."

Or:

"Corporal Henry, killed."

"And Morand?"

"Corporal Morand, wounded," said an old soldier.

"Is it serious?"

"I do not think so. Lieutenant. He got a bullet in the arm as we were moving towards the pile of logs."

Not one sergeant! Not even a corporal! All those squads which become after a time a well-beloved family to those in charge of them, a family not to be parted from without sorrow and regret—here they are deprived of their leaders, to whom they look up constantly, who watch over them, who sustain them through long and difficult hours by the mere magic of their presence. I had known each one of them so well, those I had lost today! They were the men of my choice, men for whom a single word from me was sufficient, men who had never sought to shirk their duties, accepting their task whatever it was, and fulfilling it to the very best of their powers.

Others would take their places. What would they be like? And just when I had come to know these newcomers also, they would be struck dawn too, and would disappear, or perhaps my turn would come, or that of my men! Nothing lasting, nothing that the greatest of our efforts can make really ours, even for a day. The weariness of eternally beginning over again, the sadness of acquaintances ended with a mere farewell, all the minutes of our days and nights besieged by death, death which seizes on its victims in a second's space, which selects so blindly!

Unhappy above all men is lie whose heart cherishes the memories of old affections and griefs through days unending! Close to me in the darkness someone is sobbing, sobs which cannot be choked down, which break out again and again, deep and heartbroken, bringing anguish to those who hear. I can see him who sobs, sitting in the ditch, hunched and huddled together beneath the burden of his sorrow. I know, too, why he sobs; I went up to him at once, and, as he knew me, he unburdened himself. . . .

He had a brother who was in the half sector he commanded. They had fought in the wood side by side and almost at the beginning of the business the other had received a bullet in the leg.

"He bled freely, Lieutenant; I helped him to walk; I wanted to dress his wounds. But the order came to retreat, because the Boches were advancing and were too many for us. I lifted him up and started to carry him. The bullets flew around us, many bullets. Then all at once it was as if he had been thrust forward, as if he had stumbled over a stump. He said nothing, but a second bullet had gone right through him. I had to support his whole weight then, and when I looked at him, his face was all white and his eyes staring. Still he recognized me and said: 'Jean, little Jean, leave me and get out of it.' I did not wish to do that, you may be sure. Was it possible to do such a thing?

"So I took him on my back, heavy as he was. I could not move quickly, you understand, yet even at that I seemed to hurt him. With every step I took he cried aloud in agony and did not cease pleading: 'You go on, Jean, leave me here, Jean;' and I went, yes, indeed, I went, when I saw the last blue coats disappearing over the hilltop and the Boches so close to us that I could hear the rustling of the leaves beneath their feet. It had been too much for my strength, you must understand; I had fallen to my knees and he slipped to the earth beside me. For the last time he said: 'You must go. You must not let yourself be killed because of me . . . let one of us remain alive at least.' I hung over him, I raised his head and kissed him, while all the time the bullets rained down, because the Boches had seen us and were firing at us. And then . . . I said goodbye to him . . . and then, and then I left him . . . and . . . and I left him out there . . . to die on the earth . . . in the midst of those savages. . . .

"Is he dead, do you think? What has become of him? Where is he now? Perhaps out there he is calling for me, all alone in the night. . . . I do not know, I am here; perhaps I shall never know . . . oh, yes, I can see I shall never know, never. . . .''

I have just told Porchon the story, and together we listen to those heartrending sobs.

Through the field behind us men are moving. We can hear the rustling of the dried leaves they are gathering; the falling flakes of earth from the roots they pull up; they have discovered some turnips. We remember then that so far we have eaten nothing.

It is cold. We shiver. We remain silent.

The silence is shattered by the sudden thunder of a gun. Right and left and all around other guns take up the challenge. Behind all the hilltops batteries settle down to steady work. Spurts of flame rend the darkness. Those that are far off are fugitive and faint, burning only for a second before darkness falls again; those close at hand are blindingly brilliant and still dance before the eye long after they have vanished. More and more rapid become the detonations, until all space seems filled with them. And those men who were lying down dozing, rise quickly and instinctively seek cover. Rumours are already flying about. Some say that the Boches have attacked with reinforcements under cover of darkness, that they are advancing very quickly, while our artillery is attempting to hold them back with a barrage. It is also said that we are going to counter-attack.

Counter-attack! After such a murderous, wearying day as the one we have lived through. When the exaltation of the men has died away, and they are conscious only of their aching limbs and the void in their stomachs! Counter-attack amid that darkness, with disorganized troops, without cadres, shattered! It would be both futile and cruel.

Yet if it should be necessary? If, with all the troops bivouacked in this region, there are still not enough to stay the rush of the Boches tonight? There are moments when one's duty exceeds one's powers, but when, nevertheless, it is imperative one should seek to fulfil that duty. If we go out there tonight, almost every one of us will remain out there forever and forever. Ah, well! And what of it? Shall we not go if we are ordered to do so?

The minutes fly and still no orders arrive. Little by little reflection convinces me that I have stupidly accepted for a reality what is no more than a mere rumour, arising, perhaps, from some words uttered by an unnerved man at the moment when the guns first began to speak.

Two days ago, when coming up to the outposts, we passed through the woods to reach the further edge of it. The sun was still high in the heavens, but despite the plenitude of light, the sections were separated, confused and mixed up because of the thick undergrowth. Through that undergrowth it would be necessary for the Boches to find a way, and with the darkness as another obstacle to their attack. They could never hope to get through; and, what is still more certain, they would never be such fools as to attempt to get through. If they did try, before an hour had passed they would find themselves in a hopeless mess, they would mistake their comrades for enemies, and start firing one upon the other. They know that well enough.

Our artillery is firing without doubt to cover us, to barrage the roads along which the enemy must retire, and prevent him taking up positions which he must not be allowed to occupy. I have been stupid.

At the cry of "Fall in!" which is unexpectedly issued, several of the men begin to grumble softly.

"Stop your silly tales!" I exclaim. "You know nothing of what is going to happen, and yet here you are growling already! Stop it!"

They hold their tongues and march wearily along behind me. I can feel their weariness even more keenly than my own. We are hungry and chronically in need of sleep. Each time we stop for a moment, men throw themselves down heavily beside the ditches.

We pass through Mouilly and turn to the right along a road hitherto unknown. There is a stream, dark forms bending over the water, the squelching of feet in the mud. The road rises and buries itself in the heart of some gloomy woods, but we come to a halt at the edge of them.

There we wait for daylight, acting as reserve to the advance post. I have to make certain that our connection with a company of the ——th is established. I am to find certain elements of it further along the road. Two men go out, to return only after a long interval. They have seen no one at all, and are quite confident there is no one before us.

Orders countermanded. Fall in! We go back towards Mouilly. One suspects lights behind the closed shutters. I knock at a door, and when it opens I learn that the whole company which should have been out at the advance post is there in the village! Where on earth is the phenomenon who has command of this medley? From house to house I go, to find him at last consuming a roast chicken, to which he invites me without ceremony. I receive the greatest shock of my life to find that it is L——.

"Hallo, old man! You can certainly boast of your cuisine, but is this what you call the advance posts?"

The meeting delights me, for L—— is another of my friends of the days before the war, a jovial rascal, who "cares nothing for nobody" and proves it. The information I give him—not a single guard at the approaches to the village, not a patrol on the road, not even a sentinel—leaves him thoughtful for at least two seconds. He says simply:

"I gave the orders. I suppose they weren't carried out. I must go out and see about it in a minute."

And forthwith he again sets to on the bird, happy, comfortable and serene. He really is a good fellow, but what a strange commander for a company!

Having left him, I hurry back through the village and overtake my men at the moment when the column halts opposite the last houses of the village, on the already familiar road to the Amblonville farm. The supply wagons are waiting for us there, and the issue of rations takes place without the usual disputing and grumbling. Huge fires flame clear and high. The men squat about them, bathing their hands in the warmth, watching with idle eyes the steaming pots suspended above the brazier, roasting their faces, chests and legs, while the cold night behind them freezes their backs. We receive at last greasy steaks which burn our fingers; we drink coffee, hot but innocent of sugar; the grateful warmth of which runs through our whole bodies.

Under these beneficent influences the aspect of affairs brightens a little. We may even be able to sleep a short while. My watch tells me it is only half-past one, so there is still plenty of time before daybreak. We stretch ourselves out on the earth, ignoring the fact that our clothes want to freeze to us. How icy are the nights towards the end of September! Heavy eyelids droop over eyes which retain a vision of the jumping and leaping flames of the camp fires. And sleep so grateful to our weariness steals down gently, stilling the tumults in our hearts.

A sleep well earned. . . .

"Get up!"

There is to be no sleep for us tonight; tonight we must march. Our legs do so from sheer habit, we accompany them. Here before us is a hill; we ascend it; it is steep. Here now are fields; the earth is very soft; everywhere there are holes which cause one to stumble or to fall prone with all one's weight, which is increased by the weight of the equipment.

Where are we going? No one knows.

Endless, these fields . . . apparently we are never going to arrive at our destination. Only the leader of the detachment knows where that is, and apparently he has gone and lost himself somewhere. We wander at large. The ranks break up; we march in groups, in a herd, a herd of most miserable animals. To the right: to the left: straight ahead. Our legs move onwards from sheer habit. We are out of the cultivated fields now and passing over land covered with broom, stunted pines, and brambles which merge finally into dense woods. For a long time we follow their edge, a curiously capricious edge. It brings us to the side of a road. We halt there; that is our destination.

The men, already half asleep, positively fall down. In a moment their numbed, overwearied bodies are at rest.

Scattered dark masses; a deep silence broken occasionally by loud snores.

7

The Armies go to Earth

Friday, September 25th.

Where are we? Mouilly should be over there to the right opposite the woods. I find that we have passed the last hours of the night on a plateau stretching far away behind us, sterile, and half swallowed by the forest. Before us, on the other side of the road, there are a few fields, a dip, then more forest. Towards the west is Mouilly, Rupt, the valley of the Meuse, all calm with that peace which reigns far away from the enemy. Towards the east, beyond the wood, is the last of the "Heights of the Meuse," the final barrier before the plain which they command; then the marshy Woëvre, Fresnes, Marcheville, Sceaux, Champion. Away over there somewhere are the Germans forming a human carpet at the foot of the hills, waiting a favourable moment to rush down again to the attack. They have gone south too, and captured Hattenchatel, Saint Maurice; their line runs right through the undergrowth between the old forest trees. They hold Saint Remy, Vaux-les-Palameix. Yesterday they advanced almost to the road from Saint Remy to Mouilly. Where are they this morning? And what is to be our *rôle*? We have not been told a word.

(Censored.)

. ? We are ordered: "Go there." We go there. We are commanded: "Attack." We attack. At least during the battle, we know we are fighting; we know what our immediate mission is, and knowing it, accomplish it with a better heart. But before? And afterwards? Often it is only the sound of firing close at hand or an avalanche of shells which heralds the fray.

(Censored.)

This morning the men keep constantly on the move, trotting up and down the road, hands in their pockets, tramping and stamping to restore the circulation to their frozen feet. Their moving silhouettes can be seen at a great distance, but I do not interfere. It is very cold to-day and, besides, the Boches were thrust back several miles yesterday evening; between us and them lie dense woods which cut off their view.

There is a certain gaiety and verve animating all this brisk movement in the fresh morning air.

Very soon the men gather in circles on the grass and loud bursts of laughter interrupt their conversation. Naturally, the incidents of the last fight are canvassed and, as always, when danger is no longer close at hand, made to appear a mere joke.

Yesterday's bullets were erratic and achieved fantastic results. A corporal exhibits his pocket-book split right across, the papers in which have been cut in two.

"When that bullet gently tapped me," he says, "I firmly believed I was done. My heart actually ceased to beat. As I found myself still standing upright, however, I began to examine myself. I found the hole with the pocket-book behind it. *Là! Là!* What an achievement! Quite a beautiful bit of work. But the one who got it worst, was my old woman—cut clean in two!"

From the mass of papers he draws forth a woman's photograph, displaying a long tear. Then laughs and loud-voiced pleasantries ring out:

"You are a nice sort of chap, my buck! To let your old woman take the knocks to save your own skin!"

"My boy, who can blame him? She's no further use to him!"

"Tell me, then! Seeing that it was a Boche that made the mess, doesn't it make you hot?"

The corporal, replacing the photograph in his pocket-book, replies:

"You shut up! The model of that photograph is safe enough. I can trust her a bit more than I can trust myself. Understand?"

A second man passes around two cartridges which a German bullet cut in two. Another voice says:

"It is the lieutenant that had the luck. I have seen his coat; I can't understand it at all."

A little while earlier I had shown Porchon my "wound." He agreed that I now held the record for what he called "the death graze." Fifteen days ago, during a night attack, he had the advantage over me.

On the morning of the 9th, while we were crossing the open to occupy our positions as advance posts, a bullet had struck him in the left side, passed through his bag, cutting through a tin of meat, and finally slipped down his leg. He had recovered it from the top of his boot. Later, in the middle of the fight, seeing a soldier running through the darkness towards the rear of our lines, he had seized him roughly by the arm, crying:

"Right about face at once."

At which the other, a big, helmeted brute, had jumped back, raising his bayonet. And most undoubtedly that Boche would have spitted Porchon, whose revolver was empty, had not Courret, a corporal of the company, brought the man down with a shot fired at point-blank range.

The sun, already high, gently warms the plateau. Towards ten o'clock, the cooks appear from the ravine behind us, where they have more cover from enemy eyes. They move along placidly, carrying buckets and cans, or piles of plates suspended from poles slung between them.

"Shall we eat now with the men ?" I asked Porchon.

"Not for me," he replied. "The cyclist is foraging for us as well as for the captain. He has promised to bring up his loot as soon as he can."

We wait an hour, two hours, our stomachs protesting, never moving our eyes from the ravine where the rest of the battalion is resting beside the fires. Down there is our portion of beef, rice and soup, which is so comforting when swallowed hot. It is so near, scarcely a mile away; and yet so far, since we have been stationed at the side of this road and dare not move.

"When I think," groans Porchon, "that that animal of a cyclist may at this very moment be snoring in the shadow of the trees, lying on the soft moss, his stomach well filled, and his conscience at ease. . . ."

"The cyclist," I interrupt him, "is an inferior beast, but if you had only followed my advice a short while ago, we now should also have our stomachs well filled; and the cyclist would still remain in our eyes an admirable, serviceable and dependable man, as he was this morning before this question of food arose. . . ."

"Rub it in!" snaps Porchon. "I agree that I was a fool and that is enough. Now please leave me in peace with the memory of that pot of honey I obtained at Rupt, of which you, chuckling with concupiscence, gorged at least a half, the other night before Saint Remy,

125

notwithstanding the fact that the bodies in the ditches were smelling sufficiently vilely to destroy the appetite of any normal respectable being."

At this moment, M——, the old volunteer from California, approaches, cap in hand. In tones deliberate and grave, pronouncing each syllable distinctly and meticulously, he says:

"I beg the lieutenants to pardon me. I could not, however, help overhearing a few words of your conversation, and I gather you have had nothing to eat. Before leaving for the front, I provided myself with a considerable amount of chocolate, and as some of it is still left, I should be very happy indeed. . . ."

"Not at all, M——. You must keep it. You won't be able to get any more, you know, and it is a thing of which one can never have too much."

He insists, however, with such cordiality and sincerity, that in the end we are compelled to accept half the chocolate he offers us. We divide it and carefully nibble at our respective portions to make them last as long as possible.

"Have you any tobacco?" asks Porchon when it is finished.

"You know quite well I have, also that I have no cigarette papers, since you helped me to finish up the last four this morning."

At that M—— calls aloud:

"Gabriel!"

Little Butrel rushes up to us.

"You have some cigarette papers! Pass them around."

Butrel draws from his pocket a bundle of them, and slowly unfolds the leather in which they are wrapped. Then he offers us a packet almost intact, a treasure which he extends with a smile in his blue eyes and about his thin lips. Once again we find ourselves compelled to accept another's kindness.

"I know where to find more," Butrel assures us. "There are some good friends of mine among the artillerymen over at hill X——, and they can get as many as they want."

"But if we remain out here at the advance posts for long, how will you manage then, when your friends the artillerymen are no longer available?"

"Please do not worry about that! When my cigarette-papers are finished, then I will chew or smoke a pipe. Take what you wish . . . one packet, because that will give me pleasure; a second one because that will please old grandfather. Is that not so, grandfather?"

M—— shakes his head, smiles and turns to us:

"I must tell you that he has been kindness itself to me since I rejoined. And yesterday in the woods, he saved my life. He stood up in the clearing to fire at the Boches, thus giving me time to get to the hilltop. It lasted quite five minutes, and all the time he was firing he was moving down towards them. . . . Name of a joke! but one would have said that he was playing to get himself killed."

Butrel shrugs his shoulders and begins to hum to himself. Sitting on the ground close to us, he busies himself rolling a cigarette between brown, nicotine-stained fingers. He is a splendid little soldier, this Butrel, once in the Foreign Legion, highly intelligent, straight as a die. For those to whom he takes, he would do anything, but he takes to few, however. Willingly would he die for those who succeed in winning his affections. Wherever he goes he obtains universal respect, sometimes not unmingled with fear. The hardest cases in the company, the bullies who reign over their squads by force of physical fear, give a wide berth to this thin little man, whose head scarcely reaches their shoulders. Those who attempted to molest him in the early days, suddenly found themselves uncomfortable before blue eyes which became unwontedly dark, and they flinched before the nasty threat lurking behind the cold concentrated stare.

Butrel fears neither God nor man. He enters into his proper element when under fire. Let what will happen, it finds him cheerful and all unperturbed. Joking without nervousness or bravado, he moves about as unconcerned amid a tempest of bullets as a fish swimming through the water. No one has ever seen him voluntarily take cover. When trenches are to be dug, he digs with his comrades, "he does his bit! "Nevertheless he finds the task none the less disagreeable; he doubts the utility of such labour. The unforeseen and adventurous fascinates him. Yesterday it pleased him to try and get himself killed in order to save "grandad," because long ago he had decided that grandad was a "stick," and also because it was amusing to stand upright and fire at the Boches in the clearing, precisely as if he were at target-practice. The fact that each of those Boches was armed with an automatic rifle as precise and effective as his own, Butrel ignored. He found the situation amusing, and that was enough.

He hankers after his African wars, those fights of one against five, when one plunged into the midst of wheeling horsemen teeming like wasps, or when the two 75's, set to point-blank range, spat forth their shrapnel to cut long lanes through the massed ranks of rebellious tribesmen; those nights spent beneath canvas, superb nights white with stars, rendered all the more stimulating because the surrounding blackness probably veiled a hundred ambushes; the long, still hours of sentry-go when the eyes sought to scrutinize the dark earth in fear and quaking lest the next instant might reveal the blacks stealing forward, knives between their teeth—those were days and nights after Butrel's own heart.

The present methods of warfare, the endless struggle with an invisible enemy, the shells hurled over miles of countryside, seem to him both tiresome and disgusting.

If it be true, as has been rumoured for several days past, and even more confidently affirmed this very morning, that we are going to entrench and sit down as the Boches have already done, perhaps to remain in sheer idleness with nothing better to do than to watch each other's trenches, Butrel will go to pieces, fall ill, unless . . . But the man is a very devil! As sure as the sun shines he will discover some highly intelligent way in which to quench his thirst for danger, and to amuse himself while plunging us into amazement and compelling our admiration! The style of life has not yet been created which will serve to bring Butrel down to the common standard; there is nothing sufficiently dull and depressing to extinguish the ardent flame burning within him, which makes of this little, thin, pale-faced man, with frail limbs, a soldier worthy of an epic!

Towards evening, the men scatter over the fields in quest of straw to provide at least some protection against the night. They set off quickly, spreading out towards the woods over stubble fields in which piles of corn are standing to dry; they return heavy-footed, bending beneath the weight of tremendous sheaves, the stalks of which trail out behind them like a pig-tail; a soft rustling follows their steps.

But when the darkness of the night and deep silence enfold the bivouac, loud calls suddenly ring out. Sharp brief orders bring us quickly to our feet; the sections form up with some difficulty, for the men are still to some degree in the grip of their first sleep. Then the whole battalion moves down towards Mouilly, where, so we are informed, we are going to billet.

What time is it then? Ten o'clock already! We shall have to distribute rations, settle the men in the houses and barns, cook our meat and make coffee—it will be midnight before we shall be able to get to sleep again! And we must go back to the same trenches before dawn!

There is, however, some consolation in the thought that we are going to occupy a solidly-built house, to light a fire, a fire in a real grate for a change, to stretch ourselves out perhaps beneath an eiderdown. We may even be able to take off our boots—those boots of mine, those narrow boots which I have not so far been able to replace, and which torture me inexpressibly! To be warm, to sleep without one's equipment, one's toes quite free in one's socks! . . . It certainly won't be for long, but that is all the more reason why one should hurry up and get to sleep.

Here we are at the village. An endless buzzing fills it. Supply lorries, dark wagons besieged by the darkness which the light of flickering lanterns only serves to emphasize.

The quartermaster calls to us and leads us along a shadow-filled passage-way. The earth beneath our feet is greasy and slippery.

"To the left, turn to the left. I am holding the door," exclaims our guide.

He strikes a match and lights a bit of candle he takes from a pocket at the bottom of which a hundred other similar objects are constantly accumulating. Then, raising the light, and with a magnificent gesture:

"Here you are, gentlemen! You are at home!"

Our home for that night! That which once was a home! It is no more now than a soul-less hovel, a camping-place for casual wayfarers like ourselves, who halt there for a few hours in passing to warm their frozen bodies, and then go on their way, indifferent, unregretful, leaving no trace of their hearts behind them within these old walls, old walls which enshrine the memory of hearts now still, the memory too of hearts not still, but far away in exile, who, remembering the old home, suffer!

Not long elapses before our haven is invaded. The fatigue party appears bringing up the rations for distribution. On a piece of tent canvas spread on the earth, coffee, sugar and rice are heaped in little piles. The corporal on duty, coatless, vestless, with his shirt opened to display a muscular white chest, calls up the sections one after the other. As the men approach, he indicates one of the little heaps with an almost imperceptible movement of his forefinger. Growls and reproaches move him not at all.

"That the sugar? A fat lot, isn't it? Why, you gave the third twice as much as this! It's a bit too thick!"

"There were five extra in the third," replies the corporal. "If you are not satisfied, you had better go and complain to the Ministry. That's all about it!"

During this time, Martin, a miner from the north, busies himself hacking to pieces on the table a huge quarter of beef. To assist him in this undertaking, he has no more than a pocket-knife, a pocket-knife with a safety-catch and a solid blade, which he has possessed since Vauxmarie. He tells us it was given to him by a Boche prisoner overjoyed at finding himself a prisoner, that it is a famous piece of goods, and that there is not another knife in all the company for chopping up a bit of beef to equal that Boche knife handled by him, Martin.

But Martin is a *virtuoso* where carving is concerned. He perches himself on top of the enormous mass of flesh, slices away at it with long straight strokes, hacks away savagely at resisting tendons, hunching his shoulders, clenching his teeth, flattening still more his polecat-like nose, handling the knife in a very frenzy, grunting, slashing and swearing. And when finally the task is achieved, a profoundly deep sigh of relief escapes Martin. He turns, screws up his eyes, widens his mouth with a smile distorted by the quid he is chewing, squirts a jet of brown saliva from the corner of his mouth on to the ground, and says in a self-satisfied tone, in the tone of a conqueror who, the fight finished, wishes to forget any asperity which may have marred it: "Some butcher!"

In the fireplace, vine branches hiss and splutter; the flame leaps high, lighting up the chimney plaque, the lines and reliefs of which are deeply buried beneath an accumulation of soot. The fatigue party is gone; there remain with us only the messengers and orderlies. Pannechon investigates a dish, and approaches with some pieces of smoking meat on the point of his knife. Presle wipes the table with a cloth. The others, sitting on the floor, backs to the wall and knees drawn up to chins, smoke their pipes and expectorate.

Rice soup, broiled meat with cooked rice, boiling coffee: the dinner alone is worth the march to Mouilly! And there is a bed for us! A mattress and an eiderdown! We get into it quickly. On the floor beside us our empty boots yawn wide. The dispatch-rider, ensconced in a heap of straw brought in armfuls from the barn, is sleeping heavily and fairly rocking us with his measured snoring. In our turn, we too fall asleep, well replenished, the body at ease, feet unhampered, in a dense atmosphere compounded of the fumes of burnt fat, tobacco and human beings.

Saturday, September 26th.
Beneath the big trees behind the plateau.
Another company of our battalion has taken over our position

beside the road. The morning is fresh and limpid. The men are shouting, singing, or laughing. The cooks have set themselves down near us and are busy preparing the morning meal. Around each of the fires men are sitting, absorbed and grave, holding slices of bread on pointed sticks improvised as toasting-forks, before the flames.

Toast! At once the joy and delectation of the campaigning soldier. Rusked, golden and brown, it crunches deliciously between the teeth; it melts in the mouth. There is not one of us but loves it. As soon as a fire is lit, wheresoever it may be, soon a dozen or more men are sitting around it, watching with almost touching seriousness the white bread on the end of their knives or sticks gradually assuming a delightfully warm colour, as if reflecting the flames and stealing something of their golden light. Some of the men vote for those thin slices which become crisp right through; others are all for the thick slices which, between crackling surfaces, still retain some of that steaming humidity as of loaves just withdrawn from a baker's oven. But in any shape or form, one and all love toast!

The coffee circulates. We are sitting, Porchon and I, at the foot of a giant plane tree, our backs against the smooth bole of it, our hips between two moss-covered roots which rise out of the ground like the arms of an armchair. We have stolen a branch from a cherry tree and are trying to make pipes for ourselves. "*Necessity is the mother of industry;*" and hence our labours. The making of a pipe, however, requires some skill.

Bernadot, the cook, has carved himself one which is quite a masterpiece: stem straight and drawing well, bowl smooth and deep. He has even gone so far as to carve a comrade's face out of the wood: enormous eyes in a small head, grimacing mouth, and aggressive beard, thrust well forward like the prow of a ship.

Porchon, by sheer force of will (he is scarlet, and the veins on his forehead stand prominently forth!) has so far obtained rather indecisive, but nevertheless encouraging, results. His piece of wood is slowly shaping and deepening, and unmistakably assuming something of the appearance of a pipe.

As for me, I have already been compelled to excuse three spoilt attempts by pointing out that cherry wood is hard, my knife blunt, and my fingers sore. Undeterred by these failures, however, I am starting once more, when, without the slightest warning, three high explosives burst simultaneously close to us, but rather too short. Others follow immediately, flying high, and three plumes of black smoke rise from the shattered earth a hundred yards behind us beyond the wood; range too long! Yet again come a third batch, but this time they drop far from us, exploding away to the right, uprooting a few small pines and throwing them into the air together with tremendous lumps of earth. Before us; behind us; to the right of us! It seems almost prophetic. We rise and pass through the undergrowth without haste, away to the left.

We are now out of all danger and can even afford to enjoy ourselves. One would say that the Boche artillerymen are trying to make their last shells fall in the holes dug by the first; they must be firing without any other object than to consume the regulation amount of ammunition. All that remains for us to do is to lie low until they have finished.

There is the noise of branches being thrust violently aside, of someone running over the fallen leaves, followed by a long-drawn call which resounds through the wood:

"Hullo! . . ."

Someone in our ranks cries: "Here!"

The steps approach, and very shortly the face of a man emerges from the cover. He is breathless and greatly upset.

"A doctor," he says. "Where can I find a doctor? One is wanted instantly. . . ."

"What has happened?"

The man replies hurriedly, almost incoherently:

"It is Favreau . . . cyclist of the 8th . . . a leg almost shot away about a minute since . . . the first three shells which fell behind the road . . . he is bleeding to death . . . his leg must be tied up . . . he is going out, he is certainly going out. . . ."

The doctor whose services the man has impressed, tells us when he returns that he found the wounded man in a dying condition:

"The femoral severed, the leg almost torn away. I made a ligature and got him away on an ambulance; but he will never arrive alive at Mouilly."

It is five o'clock in the evening. We are on the way to the advance posts.

We march through a narrow clearing which is no more than a ribbon of black earth between piles of dead leaves on the one side, and all-invading moss on the other. The thickets are dense and filled with a sea-green penumbra. The sinking sun is directly behind us. Its failing light streams over the moving file of men, leaving golden reflections in the tin bowls fastened to their packs. The heads of the men rise and fall with their unequal steps, causing an undulation to pass from one end of the section to the other.

There is no talking. Our feet make no noise on that moist earth, in which each nail leaves a clear imprint. Occasionally, a timid twittering is heard amid the silence, as faint and self-effacing as the failing sunrays gliding into the under- growth between the leaves of the trees.

Suddenly the surly detonation of a 75 shatters the peace; soon all the guns hidden in the wood intone a brutal chorus; the clamour envelops us; each shot seems to hurtle past with a violence sufficient to burst the gun firing it. Then a murmuring echo flies from valley to valley, gradually becoming weaker and weaker until swamped by the tremendous outburst of another salvo. To all this noise, however, we are strangely used. It seems in some curious way to mingle with the material things about us, to harmonize with them, to belong as it were to the melancholy of the dying day. We no longer jump as the guns speak; we no longer hear them; we are conscious only of the curious melody of the echoes which decrease and decrease, then sound anew with increased force, decrease again and increase again, finally to die away in a sad, tremulous murmur which spreads far away over the earth.

The evening draws on. We are approaching the edge of the wood. Beside the road lie some tattered knapsacks, some shattered bayonets; a little further on blood-stained bandages are lying on the moss, shirts, a flannel waist-band, some nameless rags, the lining of a waistcoat; further on again the body of a dead man appears stretched to his full length, face turned to the earth.

All along the edge of the clearing are shell-holes at almost regular intervals; enormous roots which have been shattered display their pale wounds. Then the shell-holes concentrate, all of them being still within the clearing, mute evidences of an admirably-directed fire. The men affirm that our artillery placed a barrage along this marked line on the evening of the 24th. They have such simple faith, these men, in the power of our guns! It may or may not have been so; personally I prefer to believe that it was so.

We halt a little before attaining the edge of the wood in a clearing surrounded by giant trees whose waving tops are lost to sight in the darkening sky.

There is a vague odour of corpses, which from time to time becomes oppressive. A few steps from our little shelter a corpse is resting against a pile of faggots in an attitude of relaxation and peace. The man was eating when killed instantaneously by a shell: he still holds in his hand a little tin fork; his waxlike face reveals no sign of pain; at his feet lie an opened tin of meat and an iron plate—an object which reminds me of those in which day-scholars at communal schools bring their dinners, and which have letters of the alphabet and figures engraved round the edge.

Flimsy and singularly draughty is our little shelter. Two pointed stakes support a branch as centre beam; other branches, cut at random and of all sizes and shapes, rest against this central beam and so make a hut. I should call it a roof without walls, decorated with disconcerting gaps, admitting the light of heaven where least expected. Someone has commenced to fill in the interstices; lumps of clay have been plastered on the framework, from the ground to halfway up; thus, when one lies down one is protected a little; we would, in fact, be quite snug if this plaster or clay covered the whole hut.

To do that will be our task tomorrow. This evening it is too late; the night is already upon us. Our last duty is to eat our cold repast, a slice of bread, a morsel of meat, which we have brought with us.

Sunday, September 27th.

I resolved this morning to go and see the adjutant whom I am due to relieve with the fall of the day. I leave the clearing towards midday, taking with me a dispatch-bearer. The weather remains the same as yesterday. The cold dawn mist has evaporated little by little; a few dewdrops still remain scintillating in the sun's rays.

A big boundary stone, covered with lichen, lies in my path; two tracks branch away from this stone. My companion, who stumbles against the stone, looks at me in doubtful perplexity.

"But there are two ways! Which is ours?"

I reflect briefly. The left of our line extends until it joins the 6th. On the right we touch the 5th, which guards the road. The road is some distance away, but that must be our direction, and so I stride along the path to the right. Ah! Ah! Stop a little . . . it is uncomfortably open just here. I did not know we were so near the edge of the wood. From a trench, two heads have arisen, as well as a hand, waved violently. The combination has proved sufficient to induce me to moderate my gait. Stooping and half running, I come up to the line of infantrymen. A joyous voice reaches me:

"Ah! there you are, Lieutenant! It is quite all right here. Only one must be careful not to show oneself because of shrapnel . . . you want to see the Adjutant? He is over there with Gendre and Lebret."

"Thank you, Lormerin. Nothing has happened during the night?"

"What do you think! All they have done is to lie still. As I tell you, we are quite blissful here . . . you will find him ten or fifteen yards away to the right."

Of course I have to cover at least fifty, stumbling over feet, and doing the acrobat to pass the men squatting in the trench. At last I see Gendre and Lebret. Gendre, who perceives me first, points out to me a man lying down.

"Don't ask him to make room for you," he says. "He would not hear you; he is dead. You will have to step over him."

Then, stooping down, he calls along the trench:

"Adjutant, the Lieutenant is here."

From the earth rises a groan; a formless mass of straw moves and rises; the head of the adjutant appears, his hair dishevelled and full of pieces of straw, his eyes weary from lack of sleep, his beard untrimmed and also full of dirt. The Adjutant seems very ill! The thinness of his cheeks is marked; a brown stain colours his eyelids; a dirty livid tint has spread over his face.

"Hullo! What is this then. Roux! Are things not going well with you?"

"I? I am about done, that is clear. Aches all over, chest stove in, a horse fever . . . it won't be long before I am sent down."

He rises to his feet, groaning again, his hands pressed to the small of his back, his chest huddled together, and seats himself on the edge of the trench at a spot which is protected by a bush.

"Sit here beside me," he says, "and I will point things out to you."

Before us extends an untilled plain bounded on the further side of the valley by steep heights. Without doubt the village lies at the bottom of the valley, but from where I am sitting it is not possible to see the houses; only one or two isolated farms. To the left, the wood forms a pronounced salient which attracts the eye. A dense cluster of pines has thrust its way right into the middle of the plain, where it forms a splash of sombre colour, opaquely green, but astonishingly fresh and distinct against the seared yellows of the surroundings.

"It is not occupied," says the adjutant. "A patrol beat it out last night; it is quite quiet this side. From here I should say it is about six or seven hundred yards distant. The Boches must be just at the edge of the valley. I should say they are a thousand yards away, so there's plenty of time to see them coming if they should take it into their heads to attack. . . . That's nothing—I am more worried about that clump of pines. I don't think it would be a bad idea to send out a few men every night to prevent the Germans stealing up in the darkness and falling right on top of us one morning. That, at least, is what I think."

He raises his forefinger as a rifle shot rings out from the enemy's lines, followed a moment later by a second and fainter detonation, echoing the first.

"Ping. . . . Pang!" he says. "That is some idiot who has been amusing himself since daybreak. Every ten minutes he sends four bullets to four different points in our line. The second should come over here."

And sure enough the Boche's rifle speaks again. The faint crack echoes while the leaden messenger flies high and whistling through the still air.

"You see what sort of a fool he is," comments the adjutant. "He must be firing at the larks! But there is something more serious I must point out to you. Follow me closely. That corner of the pines to the right there . . . you see it? . . . good! Now three fingers still to the right, there is a large bush in a hollow with some brambles before it and two solitary trees behind it. You see it? . . . Good! Well, raise your glasses and watch for a few moments. You will probably learn something."

I level my glasses and cover the bushes as directed. I see the under part of the leaves, bright and brilliant; the upper surface, sombre and dead. The upper ones are clear-cut and distinct against a sky, almost white; below there are open spaces which permit the light to filter through, but lower down, nearer the earth, the leaves are incredibly thick, presenting an impenetrable curtain.

The adjutant continues: "You will see to the left of the bush a kind of natural screen; it is there he waits."

Scarcely had he finished speaking when I saw at the precise spot indicated by him, a head surmounted by a flat helmet. It rose swiftly and disappeared even more quickly, plunging down behind the leaves. I turn towards the adjutant, who is silently laughing.

"So you have seen them!" he exclaims. "Or rather you have seen one of them . . . there are two of them hidden there. Since I first marked them this morning, they have become almost like old acquaintances; at any rate, I have been able to gather what their little plan is. The man who just showed himself is the spy. His companion is squatting on the earth beside a field telephone. All the spy can ferret out with his eyes, is transmitted *illico*. When evening comes, the telephonist will pack his little box, tuck it under his arm, wind the wire on to its bobbin and the day's work will be done. You can send men out to the nest during the night, but you won't find those cunning blackbirds there."

"But why," I ask, "do you not clear out the bush? Isn't it rather thick to let those brutes play their dirty game right under your nose?"

"Why? It is a case for consideration, you understand. If I fire upon those two Boches, within five minutes shrapnel will be hailing down upon us, and I am certain to have wounded and killed upon my hands. I prefer to keep my men well hidden and undisturbed while the Boche twists his neck out of joint, running the risk always of picking up a bullet, without discovering more than the tail of a blue coat. But all the same, if you are here tomorrow and the bush is still occupied, you can fire if you will, and perhaps you will be right. Today, however, I am ill, and, with your permission, I vote for tranquillity."

"We'll let it go at that, on the understanding that not one of your men shows himself while it is still light. You are not permitting smoking, of course? "

"I do know at least a little about the business," answered the adjutant with melancholy. "If I could only scotch one or two of them to cure them I would be content. Ping! Pang! do you hear it, there's my brother idiot recommenced! Ah, well, let it pass. Peace until tonight, anyhow! I am going to crawl into my straw again."

A shell bursting in the clearing heralds my return to the little shelter. The quartermaster calls out from the interior:

"At least, Lieutenant, no one can say you don't announce yourself! Something like a gong that! "

He turns his back to a veritable volley of shells which falls into the open space. The fracas is terrific, fragments of metal fly in all directions before the opening to the shelter with a remarkably unpleasant "frrt."

"Oh! Oh! "cries Porchon. "Those are 105's. They are serving us well!"

"If they continue," jokes the quartermaster, " they are going to demolish our little house. This roof is only proof against 77's. Look out!"

Yet another avalanche behind us. A volley of fragments strikes the branches sharply, followed immediately by an immense creaking and cracking, a violent agitation of high branches, and the reverberating crash of a tree falling.

We are about to be called upon to endure a scientifically regulated bombardment. The men are not pleased. I put my head outside to see them lying upon the moss, scattered in widely-separated groups of two or three. They all have their kit on their back and await unmoved the end of this sprinkling.

The shells in their fury shatter the undergrowth, laying bare the black soil beneath. They create an ear-splitting din, flying across the clearing, now growing distant, now returning to burst directly over our heads, tearing down entire trees, hurling roots into the air, scattering the thicket to the four winds. But they strike blindly and unseeing like maddened, unintelligent brutes; their fury, which should be terrible, becomes simply grotesque, a mere impotent frenzy.

When the inferno about us dies down a little, one can hear the shrapnel mewing over the first line of our section. And when I remember the adjutant and his extravagant precautions, I feel an almost irresistible desire to laugh.

The moment comes when, the last shell having sent its leaden charge over us, complete silence again falls over the woods. There follow several seconds of inaction, during which one becomes conscious of muscles still instinctively shrinking, of the throbbing of the blood in the arteries. Then here and there heads pop up. Soon the men are sitting up ridding themselves anew of their equipment, rising to their feet, and stretching themselves. That little interlude is ended!

Night overtook me in the cutting while I was leading my *poilus* to relieve the adjutant. Beneath the trees darkness reigns supreme, a blackness that seems almost palpable, which our eyes strive vainly to pierce. It is as if a wall surrounds us which advances with each step forward we take; it amazes us that we do not strike either feet or face against it; we thrust forth an arm to touch it, but we never succeed in touching it, for it recedes and vanishes before our very finger-tips. Always beyond our reach, yet always there before us, imprisoning us.

I halt my men at the edge of the wood. The shadows here are less dense. Immediately before us is the unpeopled space of the open. As one by one we pick out the vague forms of the bushes, it almost seems as if they had moved to look at us before recomposing themselves to slumber.

I jump down into the trench where I detect a man lying down and grasp his shoulder, but he does not move. I shake him, more and more violently, and all unprotestingly he permits me to do so. How the fellow sleeps! Then I bring my face so close that I touch his. Ugh! ...A skin clammy and cold, over a deadly soft flesh. This is a corpse! The ghastliness of the encounter sends a clutching to my heart. Carefully I step over the body and advance a few paces, calling softly. After a time a voice replies. I walk towards it, my feet rustling the straw; near me I hear invisible movements—now at least I am in the midst of the living!

"What section is this?" I ask.

"The third section, Lieutenant."

"I require a man to lead me to the Adjutant."

"Present! Letertre."

"Good! Let us get out of the trench or we'll never make progress. I will follow you."

While we march along, whipped by clusters of leaves, torn by embracing thorns, Letertre questions me:

"You did not stumble over a dead body before you chanced on us, did you? . . . Yes! Ah, well! That is number one point they have marked. There are plenty of other bodies further along between the 6th and us; but coming from the clearing and descending into the trench, you fall directly on top of that one, who is the last of our file. You should then turn carefully to the right. Count thirty or thirty-five steps. . . . Having done so, you will find a shirt we have spread on the ground. That represents the second marked point and means that you should take a half-turn to the left. Just there the line advances a little. Walking straight ahead from that point, you would enter the wood and lose yourself. Hallo! Here is the shirt."

A faint white blot lay at our feet; had the blackness been less opaque, it might have been a ray of veiled moonlight filtering through the trees. Letretre continued:

"You are following me, are you not, Lieutenant? Now twenty-five more steps bring us to a second body. The journey is almost ended then, provided one does not stray away to the right. Ten yards or so alone separate us from the second section. By daylight, of course, it is all very simple, and one can walk boldly ahead; but if these little precautions are neglected by night, one may lose oneself a hundred times over in the cursed forest. . . . Now where is that body? It is impossible to pass it without knowing. You understand? . . . It is difficult to see. Ah, there it is! This way a little or you will tread right on it—he is lying all over the place. All right? . . . Good! We must keep well to the right here or we shall find ourselves up to the eyes in those brambles, which appear to be nothing from here, but which, nevertheless, rise higher than your head. And now. Lieutenant, we have reached our destination. I will go back again if you have no further need of me. .

. . Goodnight!"

I find the adjutant still buried in the straw. Faithful Lebret, who cooks for him and never leaves his side, has thrown over him a covering found at the bottom of a cupboard back in Mouilly. I can distinguish the vague whiteness of it in the trench.

"I am sorry you should have come all the way up to relieve me," says the adjutant. "It was careless of me not to explain to you the marks and signs to keep you on the proper road when you were here earlier. But I was in such a rotten condition, I did not think of it. Moreover, you know, I was no longer expecting you."

While addressing me, he is shivering with fever and the cold. All the time he talks his teeth chatter audibly.

"Just get your men ready," I reply. "I am going to fetch mine up immediately. With the best will in the world, however, I can't place them in five minutes."

"Listen!" he says, in the same shaky voice. "I would much prefer you to wait for daybreak. The night is drawing on; I have made all dispositions, and, after all, one place is about as good as another. I would rather remain here a few hours longer than go through the muddle and upset which it will be impossible to avoid if we arrange the relief now. And I am sure my men are one with me in this."

"I agree most willingly. But it is your turn to pass into reserve, you know!"

"Bah! Everything is quiet. The Boches won't come out of their holes. *Pristi!* What a night! Darker than the throat of a wolf. . . . Until the morning then, Lieutenant?"

"I shall be back shortly before daybreak. Roux."

Monday, September 28th.

Before the dawn this morning, the whole battalion was relieved. We retired to the second line a mile to the rear. We are still close to the Boches, however, so close in fact that this cannot be regarded as a real rest; in case of attack we must sustain the shock together with the first line. Although, however, it cannot justly be described as more than a half-rest, it is, none the less, not to be despised. Hidden deep in the forest, we are invisible even to reconnoitring aeroplanes; we can come and go freely, lounge outside the trench, return to it only in case of an alarm.

Whistling, my hands in my pockets, I stroll as far as a neighbouring crossroad. I find the captain there, smoking his eternal cigarettes rolled in extraordinarily long cigarette-papers. He points out to me a dead

German stretched out lower down the slope. Someone has covered the man's face with a handkerchief, neatly folded his greatcoat and placed it beside him. The man's unbuttoned waistcoat reveals a blood-stained shirt. His hands, very white now, still seem to be supple and living: they have but just relaxed after the final death struggle; they are not the stiff and rigid hands of those who have been dead many hours and are already turning to dust.

"He has just died?" I ask.

"Five minutes ago! He was found in the woods and brought here just as we arrived. He fell in an assault three days ago, and his men were unable to take him back with them. Three days and three nights lying between the lines! He was dying as much from cold and exhaustion as from his wounds when one of our patrols found him at daybreak. A fine, big fellow, isn't he?"

He was indeed, and well groomed, too. I had not noticed that at first. His uniform was a shade darker than that of an ordinary private; his trousers were fastened at the knees; his high, soft leather boots revealed a pair of muscular legs.

"An officer?" I ventured.

"Lieutenant of reserve, and probably commanding a company. But I hadn't either the time or inclination to question him. He had asked in French for an officer speaking German. They brought me. When I came up, he was lying beside the trench, eyes filming, lips blue, dying then but perfectly clear in his mind. He entrusted to my care some personal papers and letters which he requested me to forward to his people, advising them of his death through the intermediary of the Red Cross. He dictated their address and thanked me; then he let his head fall and was dead without even a sigh. A real man, that!"

I regained my trench sunk in melancholy thought. No longer did I see the forest about me, beautiful in its last and most splendid garb. Here is the trench, a narrow ditch between two vertical walls of earth. A few scattered men are fast asleep at the bottom of it. The night will see it peopled from end to end. And away beyond the edge of the wood there are more and still more trenches like this, one and all filled with soldiers. Further away, over the plain, are other trenches, but they are filled with soldiers who are not like ours. We dig, but over there, where the men in the spiked helmets teem, they too dig, and more and better than we do. I have watched them at work, these human moles.

Along the Cuisy valley, I one day watched them through my glasses for hours, and saw them handling pick and shovel with a vigour that knew no pause or slackening. As soon as they can safely call a halt, the Boches instantly dig their holes and take refuge in them. If they advance, they entrench themselves, to ensure continued possession of the ground they have won. If they retreat, yet again they entrench in order the better to repulse the assaults hurled against them. And day by day I see, facing our lines, these entrenchments grow and extend, escalading hills, plunging into valleys, crossing plains; deep trenches with their parapets stark and clear against the sun, with their meshed miles of barbed wire rising high before the machine-gun emplacements.

First we checked them, then we rolled them back. In the ensuing pause, both armies are now regaining their breath. Panting from their recent exertions, too weary yet once again to hurl themselves against the barrier we present and pass onwards over our bodies, they have set themselves down on the soil of France, which they still occupy.

And that they may remain in greater security and comfort, they have set up their barriers against us. Ingeniously, methodically, they accumulate and multiply the obstacles. Nothing is left to chance; every yard of ground they hold will have its guard of rifles; behind each hilltop there will be big guns. There is no gap, no weak point. From Flanders to Alsace, from the North Sea to the frontiers of Switzerland, one immense, stupendous fort is being created, which we must shatter before we can pass.

When may we hope to pass it? October is already here; very shortly now we shall have the storms, the snows, the rains, all those elements that combine to discount mobility. If we are to hold on, we must dig as they do; must learn to construct shelters of branches with sand-bagged roofs. We must teach ourselves to wait without weariness through the long, grey days and the black, cold, endless nights. It is going to be a hard business! When one is hungry, one can tighten one's belt; when idle, write letters or dream; when cold, light a fire, or stamp one's feet, or thrust hands into pockets, or breathe on one's fingers. But when the heart, growing heavy, begins to sink into one of those unfathomable seas of despondency and despair; when one's sufferings arise not from things physical but from oneself, where may one look for succour then? How escape those black hours? The close of a lugubrious day represents the last word in depression. Is not the dying away of a day, of one more day, always sad, with the light fading regretfully as though pregnant with memory of so many long hours of light?

142

Pondering these things, I forget the Boches dug in opposite us, the watch we should keep, the bloody struggle that must inevitably ensue sooner or later when we shall have acquired both the will and the strength to overthrow them and trample them to the dust. For a great trial is descending upon me, and it is one I cannot escape—the tremendous struggle against the perils and lurking evils of idleness. On the very threshold, I already tremble at what lies ahead. May I always be on my guard against the insidious ambushes before my footsteps, and find myself on the return of the hour of action with all my strength and courage undiminished!

Two shells falling shatter my reflections. A man drops on to his back crying: "M——!"

There is something for me to do here, and no mistake. Towards the cross-roads some horses burst into shrill neighs of fear, their drivers swearing and loudly cracking their whips. Then two grey wagons appear, tilting on to two wheels as they swing towards the trench, the drivers lashing the spume-whitened horses with all their might. Into the woods they plunge, wheels thundering, creaking, rattling. They are the supply wagons, galloping madly for safety. The fatigue party will have several miles further to walk tonight!

"Everyone take cover in the trench! "These shells descend upon us without warning. I was watching one of my men ramming the tobacco into his pipe at a moment when two more burst right on top of us: the hissing shell, the grimace of the man and the plunge he made, the hail of bullets amid the branches, combined to create a single impression of an attack evil and unforeseen. It is too swift; the instinctive reflex action one's body makes to protect itself occurs too late. The shell which comes with a shriek to herald its approach is a very different thing; that which explodes immediately over your head without the faintest sign of warning is both more dangerous and nerve-shaking; for a long time following these unexpected explosions the hands continue to tremble.

There they go again! Is the visitation going to endure the whole day? Every ten minutes or so we are being sprinkled with shrapnel, followed by high-explosive shells, which make the earth tremble and quiver. And they are all 77's. The firing too is direct, as a rifle is aimed, and therefore almost unbearable. Judging by the tremendous speed at which their shells arrive, they must be fired from very close at hand; the Boches must have brought a couple of guns up into their first line and are operating beneath our very noses as it were. I would not mind betting, indeed, that they have planted the two ugly little beasts right in Saint Rémy itself! Our outposts will have marked and ranged them at the very first shot, however. And so, thanks to a superb and perfected system of communication, it will not be long before they are either demolished or muzzled. Meanwhile, I know quite well their savage barking will continue until the Boche gunners become tired of the game. That is a thorn in our flesh of which we cannot for the moment rid ourselves, and so we must remain until nightfall, huddled up in the trench, our knees up to our chins, denied the liberty and freedom that lie beneath the trees.

When night does arrive at last, it finds us completely exhausted—backs aching, legs incredibly stiff. Porchon and I have been tightly jammed together at the bottom of the trench—a place not remarkable for spaciousness, and made more uncomfortable by the sharp stones littering the ground. My revolver stuck in my ribs; my flask in my hip; one of Porchon's knees was in my stomach. To sleep on the hard ground, good! We have been well broken in to that. But here the accumulation of discomforts becomes almost unendurable. An involuntary movement and Porchon groans woefully, for now he has both my knees in his stomach. What a posture to be in! What a hole to find oneself in! As soon as one moves, one crushes one's neighbour; as soon as he moves, he crushes you. Leave the trench and lie down on the dead leaves? But there are the shells, and there is the cold to penetrate to your very marrow, and keep you always conscious of your own misery!

I have never before, however, encountered any trench quite as bad as this one. The time draws on; I woo sleep and call myself a fool for my pains. Still, of many evils choose the least and pay the shot as cheerfully as possible. So I wedge all my equipment, including my revolver, flask, glasses, map-case, between my stomach and my thighs, and in this way relieve the strain on my back. Afterwards I extract the stones which project unreasonably and fling them carefully over the parapet. Things are slightly improved by these manoeuvres, and, affectionately clasping my miscellaneous collection to my bosom, I fall into a doze.

Tuesday, September 29th.

The aforesaid two filthy little guns have been harassing us nearly all day. This evening, however, we evacuated that shell-riddled and particularly undesirable corner of the landscape. Already Mouilly is behind us, and here is Moulin-Bas, the stream filled with rushes, the sea of slender trees, the large farmhouse with the tiled roof near the crossroads. A sunset crimson, but cold, marking the end of a glorious winter's day. The lines of the heights are cut stark and clear against a soft sky, darkening little by little, as though under protest. At the end of the road a spire uplifts its delicate silhouette; in a field are some 75's, which, in contrast with the houses, seem no more dangerous than pretty little playthings.

Halt at the approach to the village, while commands pass down the lines.

"Dress by the right! . . . Ground arms! . . ."

Some of the men sneer a little. At the end of the section preceding us, a fair little man with crimson cheeks, whose *puttees*, very badly rolled, sag over his boots, taps his pipe lightly against the stock of his rifle, places it in his pocket, spits a last time, and growls:

"There you are! We are certainly going to sign peace tomorrow! We might be re-entering barracks after a march. Tighten straps! Heads erect! Fasten your eyes on the clock tower! Ah, but joking apart . . . we are at war!"

The corps commander in person appears on horseback, and he is not well pleased with things:

"No smartness about them . . . slovenly . . . nothing military. . . ."

With arms ported and marching as if on parade we enter at last into the promised land. As we pass each corner of a road, a company debouches and hurries off to its quarter. The 7th turns to the left and goes off towards Rupt.

The men are pleased with their billets, and say so. The barns are spacious and warm and full of hay. The pork-butcher's wife who sells the pig's-head brawns, those brawns covered with a golden jelly which positively glide down one's throat, has her shop in the middle of our domain. And twenty yards beyond the last house, the stream spreads out to form a peaceful pond, preserved and kept clean by a mere trickle. Could one ask for anything better in which to wash one's linen?

We are already installed, rifles racked along the sides of the barn, when the battalion adjutant thrusts his face and pipe around our door. I shall not attempt to set down the language that ensued; but, briefly, we had to un-install ourselves. Farewell, thou golden-jellied brawn, farewell!

We are set down for duty in the vicinity of a sawmill. Logs of timber of equal lengths, planks already sawn, are piled outside the sheds.

We have to set a sentry, bayonet fixed, to help the cooks preserve the timber from the depredations of those frail mortals who might be tempted to help themselves and merrily burn the mill's stock. A temptation not difficult to understand!

"And now," says Porchon to me, "we have got to fit ourselves out again! There must surely be some precious things about here; but perhaps in an hour or so they will carry them off."

There ensues the usual chase for rations. For that business one should possess the scent of a hound to worry out obscure corners; and diplomacy, to reach the hearts of these peasants and overcome their hesitation—for they always hesitate, never freely parting with whatever they may have for sale, hoping that another purchaser may come along and offer more than you are offering.

A freemasonry which tends to mutual benefit exists among campaigning comrades:

"Look here! Down that lane, the third house to the left, the one with the green shutters, there is an old woman who sells eggs. . . ."

Let us go and investigate! The old woman, horrible to look upon, dry as the seared vine, toothless, filthy, untidy strands of grey hair hanging about her face, raises her arm to the sky and calls upon the Holy Virgin to witness that she has nothing, nothing at all. . . . We mention a price, a ridiculous, extortionate figure. It is plain magic; the arm drops instantly; her voice descends an octave; and then the old miser glides along a passage-way thick with fowl-droppings, bends her body to pass through a low doorway, emerges with caution, carrying something in her apron. And when she approaches again, half a dozen eggs are clutched in her claw-like hands—they are white as milk in contrast with her dirty, lined palms. They are still warm when she drops them into our pockets. In a lowered voice, with lips stiffly drawn over her bare gums, she says:

"Do not tell anyone about it. Perhaps I shall have some more for you when my hens have laid. But don't breathe a word about it. Mind, not a word!"

Porchon has discovered some plum jam. Jam?—it is rather a compound of quinces scarcely sweetened.

"I paid seven *sous* a quarter for this mixture," he informs me. "The pigs who sold it to me had two enormous copper cans full of it on their counter, and they emptied them in half an hour at the same price."

The robbers! Before the war, these quinces were left to ferment

146

in hogsheads. Each hogs-head gave a few pints of brandy at forty *sous*, and the pulp of the fruit was then thrown into the fire. It is not an augury of good times ahead!

We dine with an old Alsatian woman, a neat clean old woman, rosy and well preserved. She wears a bonnet, round and very white, so white that never before in the whole Meuse district have I seen one quite so chic and prepossessing. A doorway of bricks, newly washed, clean and as red as one's face after a wash in cold water; furniture which shines as does the top of the table covered with brown oilcloth. Above the sink a brass bracket reflects the light of our lamp and sends a pencil of light through the darkness.

"Cabbage soup!" announces Presle, "and after that we have roast fowl."

Oh! that roast fowl! A consumptive hen, a lamentable thing, lying on its back in the middle of an immense dish. To the head with its closed eyes was attached a body about as big as a fig, and the claws, which Presle had neglected to remove, were crisp, black and contracted as though in agony.

"It is certainly not a Bresse fowl," explains Presle in self-extenuation. "And, at the same time, I believe that her flirtations must have made a long-distance walker of her before I wrung her neck. All the same, it is fowl."

After dining, I inspect a collection of shoes which the cyclist has picked up, I know not where. It is difficult to make a selection: these are too broad, those are too long; some are already worn; others, which fit exactly and appear on first sight to be made of soft yet solid leather, unexpectedly reveal a long cut. At length I choose a pair with welted soles, newly clumped, of which the cyclist says:

"I guarantee them for six months without repair. Lieutenant. They will carry you to the end of the campaign, of that you can be certain."

"Amen! "I replied.

We go out arm in arm, Porchon and myself. The night is not very dark. The piles of planks near the sheds rise in dark, geometrical masses. The village to the right is lightless and still; away to the left, towards the cemetery, a pale mist broods over the fields. An undulating line of willows marks the course of the stream which they veil. The line continues to the foot of an abrupt slope, rising to the south-east like a gigantic wall.

"Where are you taking me?" asks Porchon.

"Just wait a little and you will see."

We walk in silence, occasionally burying our feet in heaps of soft ashes, which mark the spots where braziers have burnt.

"Point of direction, that isolated house," I explain, after a time. "There are some steps and an iron railing. Hold on to me, old man! You are going to see what you are going to see."

I take the stone steps in three jumps and knock at the door. Children's voices die abruptly to silence, a step sounds over the floor, the latch clicks, and the door opening wraps us in a gust of warm air.

We are in a smoky kitchen, dimly lit by a single candle placed on the table. From a line across the room hang stockings, handkerchiefs, swaddling clothes, drying above a stove. The chairs, scattered here and there, are all encumbered with a heterogeneous collection of things—a wash-hand basin, a pair of pants, dirty dishes.

Beneath one's feet one crushes certain soft things, remains of food probably, or chewed tobacco.

Our host is still a young man, sickly, pale, thin as a skeleton, his moustache and hair light-coloured. He offers us his hand with a tired gesture; it is a feverish hand, in which one can discover no bones, but only cartilages; and which, when you release it, leaves some of its moisture on your palm.

"We have been awaiting you," says the man. "My wife has prepared beds for you in that corner there, against those sacks of bran."

The woman, who is also a blonde, but swollen and paunched, leaves her chair near the stove, shakes off three or four urchins hanging to her skirts, and raises the candle from the table.

We can see clearly now. Along the sides of the plastered wall sacks are stacked. In these sacks the miller has placed a plentiful litter of straw, and, what is still more important, of an even depth all over. On the top of the straw she has placed a feather mattress, blankets and sheets. Tonight we're going to have sheets, a real bed, a complete bed. We're going to undress ourselves, to install ourselves between two sheets, wearing nothing but our shirts. I steal a glance at Porchon from the corner of my eye; his face plainly expresses his unfeigned delight and joy.

Suddenly he turns towards me, places his hand on my shoulder, and regarding me with warm, affectionate eyes, says:

"You brick!"

Our bed that night was a thing never to be forgotten. Undressed in a twinkling of an eye, we plunged into its depths. And instantly it

148

wrapped us from head to foot in a sweet, gentle embrace. Then in our turn, little by little, detail by detail, we took possession of it. There was no end to our surprise; each second produced some new discovery; in vain we sought with the whole of our body for some hardness, but there was no corner that was not soft and warm.

Our bodies, which remembered all the stones of the field, all the gaps in the soil, and the greasy humidity of the woods, the harsh dryness of the stubble-fields; our bodies, bruised by nights of bivouac, by the straps of our equipment, by our shoes, by the weight of the knapsack, by all the harness of wanderers who know no roof—our bodies at present were unable swiftly to accustom themselves to so much softness and pleasure, all at one and the same time. And we broke into shouts of laughter; we expressed our enthusiasm in burlesque phrases, in formidable pleasantries, each one of which provoked new laughter which knew no end. And the man laughed at seeing us laugh, and his wife laughed, and the urchins laughed; the hovel was full of laughter.

Then the woman stole out, and when she returned she was escorting five or six of the neighbouring villagers. And all these women, too, watched us laughing, and exclaimed in astonishment and chorus at this phenomenal spectacle—two poor devils so far scorned by death; two soldiers of the great war who had fought often, had suffered much, delirious now with happiness, laughing with the abandonment of children because they were sleeping for that one night in a bed!

Wednesday, September 30th,

A happy party are we, up above Amblonville valley. A tempered sun, a sky intensely blue, with a few little white clouds idling by. Near me on a slope the men are digging a trench; I have brought them almost up to a summit where clay gives way to chalk. Their task is easy; the picks loosen huge flakes of soft stone which scarcely adhere to each other, and which part at a single stroke. Earth such as this does not blunt or spoil the tools, and the work proceeds without pause. It is not like clay which sticks whatever one may do, compelling one constantly to scrape pick and shovel with a knife or a sharp stone.

Far away below, in a meadow beside a stream, the cooks have lit their fires. About *pots-au-feu* which crown the flames are gathered a few men in blue and red. The whole picture is so clear-cut and distinct that by concentrating my attention I am able to recognize each one of these pigmy-like men.

A few yards from the stream, and because camp-buckets are heavy to carry when they are full of water, Lebret is holding his particular assizes. The adjutant is squatting close to the flame, and Gendre, stripped of his equipment, and in his vest, is balancing himself and walking on his hands.

In the middle of the meadow, I can easily distinguish the cooks of my section. The man who is kneeling down and puffing at the green wood and half vanishing from time to time in the smoke, is Pinard, hairy among the most hairy in the company; Pinard, who grumbles incessantly, but who always works like any other four men put together. That other, bending so solicitously over certain dishes, is Fillot, the fatigue corporal, inspecting some particularly choice morsel which he has carefully placed aside before the distribution of rations, as every corporal of ordinary intelligence and respectful of traditions, does do.

Further to the right, on the other side of the road which descends from our hill to rejoin the main road, the captain is sitting on an old tree-trunk and drawing designs in the dust with the point of his lance, chatting at the same time with the doctor, who is standing near him. Behind them lies an overturned, rusty plough.

I have carefully sharpened the point of my pencil, and, using my map-case as a desk, I scribble a few letters. A few words only:

"In good health; best wishes."

I cannot permit myself to tell them all that is in my heart. And why should I tell them? Shall I repeat again and again what is in my heart:

"Please write me. I have received nothing from you since I set out. I feel all alone and that is hard."

I know well that not a day has passed without their sending me words of courage and tenderness, in the hope that they may find me, that I may read them, and that by them my courage will be strengthened and sustained. I should be ill-advised to destroy that hope. I must wait and wait, consecrating all my powers to preserving intact that confidence which I so essentially needed, which up to the present moment has never deserted me. So my pen moves swiftly, setting down those banalities which nevertheless are so eagerly awaited:

"I am in good health: Best wishes!"

I have ended; my pen flies no longer. But that melancholy I experienced a few hours ago is still with me, and gradually it increases, tempting me to abandon myself to it entirely. Most miserable of men! Am I too weak, then, boldly to face the crisis and to overcome it with an equal mind? It would indeed be true courage to grapple with it and triumph over it; the worst form of self indulgence would be merely to pander to it and take melancholy pleasure in my own suffering.

I jump to my feet, rush down the slope, leaping the shell-holes, and go from fire to fire, questioning, joking, inspecting the various dishes.

"Good-day, Roux! What are you grilling there?"

"You do not know, Lieutenant? Is it possible? It is a biscuit, pure and simple. Try them. But dip it in water before toasting it, if you want to make it really toothsome. Or dipped in milk, it is delicious. Better still is it if you split it in two and make a butter sandwich of it. In the early days, we were able to get fresh butter from the Amblonville farm. But today! . . ."

Presle, advancing with tremendous strides, comes running towards us from the top of the hill.

"I was looking for you, Lieutenant," he exclaims. "I thought you were still up there. A cyclist has just come to say that you are wanted at the paymaster's office. They are sending for all the officers, one after another. . . . It must be your turn now!"

The paymaster? Of course, this is the last day of the month!

And I am in such frame of mind that I am not at all ill-pleased I should have to go alone. Striding rapidly down the road, I amuse myself watching the larks settling and pecking away in the dust. They let me approach them until I am able to distinguish their sharp, black eyes, their slender claws and their quaint little crests. Then, with a flutter of feathers, a stroke of their wings, they flash away almost from beneath my feet. But they do not go far; lightly they glide down into the nearest field, perch on the top of some molehill, and with head on one side, tranquilly and mockingly watch me. When I have gone on far enough, they return to the road and settle on the spot from which I drove them.

It is midday when I leave the paymaster's office, my money safe in my pocket. I discover that the walk has made me hungry, but the prospect of returning to the valley to eat the inevitable boiled meat and cooked rice—it will already be more than half cold—does not please me. I find the prospect not at all inviting. A sudden longing for dishes dainty and rare, for savoury dishes to be masticated at leisure, seizes me. My liberty of the morning, the comparative freedom of action of which only a short time remains to me, is in itself so unusual and pleasurable a sensation, that I feel the occasion demands some adequate form of celebration. Had I known in advance what was going to befall, I would have made all the essential arrangements, fittingly to mark the occasion. Being a victim of the unforeseen, no choice remains to me; I must extemporize. And since the abnormal yearning for meats tender and juicy obsesses me, I must seek, solitary and alone, to satisfy it.

Fortune is good to me. A white house with sunlit *façade* attracts my attention. On a garden seat near the door an old man sits, placidly warming himself in the sunshine. No complications bar the way to complete mutual understanding. He invites me to step into a perfect little kitchen; and there his daughter-in-law makes me an omelette never to be forgotten. This is followed by smoked ham, which she cuts specially for me. I eat like a glutton; near my left hand reposes a long baton of new bread, to which I help myself at will. Again and again the old man replenishes my glass with Toul wine, rosy, sparkling and dry. The fresh ham on my plate has a sheen; before me, near my glass, in which the bubbles foam, there is a stone jar of golden jam.

And when the ham at last only too obviously reveals the force and verve of my attack, when the jam-pot is half emptied, I light my pipe with a sigh of deep satisfaction. It is I who have enjoyed these delicacies, I alone. Through half-closed eyes I watch the blue smoke mounting to the rafters, swamped in a sensation of physical well-being, and evoke a picture of my comrades back in the valley, sitting down to the eternal stew and cooked rice—something of remorse, I must confess it, mingles with my self-satisfaction!

Thursday, October 1st.

We received a surprise yesterday evening on returning to our quarters—the regimental band has been playing Two-Steps and dreamy *valses* on the village green. We had just unbuckled our straps before the barns when the first strains burst forth. The immediate effects of this unwonted clamour were somewhat remarkable. Less than a minute after one of the men had cried "There's a band!" the German centre had been broken! A minute later and we had made eighty thousand prisoners. By the time I arrived on the scene, the Russians were in Berlin. Outside the sawmill I met an old *dame* who informed me with an air of great mystery: "That the *Kaiser* was dead of a stroke, but no one would be allowed to say anything about it until tomorrow!"

On investigation, however, I learn that this concert is not intended to celebrate a manifestation of national joy, but is the result of an idea of our major. Battalion orders handed to me as I leave duly enlighten me. I read that: "The appearance of the regiment is slovenly"... that it "shows only too plainly the effects of a prolonged stay in the wooded regions where man displays a tendency to revert to a condition of nature"... that "it is essential to return by degrees to a more healthy and regulated style of living." So apparently a reasonable ration of music, Two-Steps and dreamy *valses*, is destined to tame for ever that ancestral savagery in us which the war has awakened.

And this morning at daybreak We are departing from the village once again to bury ourselves in those wooded regions where man becomes a wolf!

It is misty and the leading files of the battalion vanish from sight in a white cloud. The company preceding us is no more than a moving mass in which only the rifle barrels swaying above a crowd of heads can be distinguished. At a lesser distance forms are visible, all dull grey, but it is only when quite near that We can recognize different colours in the uniforms and see the men's breath as white puffs which quickly dissolve.

Amblonville, Mouilly, and then a narrow ravine. The slope we are mounting is covered with shrubs, hazel, cherry trees, dwarf oaks and a few big trees; at the bottom of the ravine is a lake of greenness which has retained its freshness despite the autumn. In it countless shell-holes form miniature archipelagos. The opposite slope is covered with a thinly-sown wood of pines.

The fog has disappeared and unveiled the sky. Idly I watch several of our men lounging near the pines. Three of them are sitting playing cards and smoking, two others standing behind them watch the game closely, commenting from time to time. A little higher up the slope a man is lying flat on his stomach, supporting his chin on his hands, and reading absorbedly, digging his toes in the soil the while.

I was watching, and I saw in all its brutal horror the thing that came to pass. A shell swept over the edge of the hollow, passing so close above us that we felt its breath in our faces, and dropped plumb in the centre of the peaceable group of card-players. We heard them cry aloud; then beheld two of them running madly. In the crater made by the shell the black smoke hung, and drifted for some time; little by little it disappeared. And when it was gone we saw a human trunk in bloody rags hanging between two branches of a pine. A second wounded man lay on the earth beside the mutilated legs of his comrade, and he was waving his arms and screaming. The stretcher-bearers came up at full speed.

I can see them now at the bottom of the ravine, carrying the wounded man on a stretcher; can follow their course through the high grass. And while they are making for the road, other men dig a grave in the hole dug by the shell. In a few minutes all is over; no deep hole is necessary to receive those poor human fragments!

I watch them get the soul-sickening *débris* down from the tree, and gently place it in the hole, together with the two legs: then the earth falls in heavy lumps. Two branches to form a cross; a name, a date. How simple it all is! After our departure tomorrow others will come as smiling and indifferent before the constant menace of death as ourselves. And perhaps near that grave which the shell dug, other card-players will seat themselves on the moss, and throw down their cards and laugh amid the fragrant bluish smoke of their pipes.

Friday, October 2nd,
To Mouilly, all alone, hands in my pockets. I have been ordered to supervise the clearing up of the village, have all the rubbish buried, and hunt looters and deserters out of the houses.

I conscientiously accomplished this delicate mission of marshal, dustman, and police officer. I formed several fatigue-parties, each with a definite task. I sent out patrols and walked up and down the streets myself.

The results are praiseworthy. Bones, empty meat tins and other indescribable things have disappeared beneath the earth. The roadway has been well brushed with birch brooms. Never before, not even in pre-war days, has the village been so aggressively clean. It looks as if it has been an object of tender care. Even the shattered roofs and holes in the walls now appear less desolate. Perhaps, however, I look on these things with a prejudiced eye; I am rather pleased with myself and my men; maybe that I exaggerate.

A dozen soldiers are kneeling side by side before a trough, bending over the soapy water, washing their linen in silence. But where is the Washing and the babbling washerwomen of a year before? One hears nothing now but the slapping of palms against the Wet clothes, and the noise of the trickling water wrung from them.

"Hullo, Pannechon? Almost finished?"

Pannechon looks up. Still kneeling and resting his hands on the inclined plank before him, he turns his head to look at me.

"Yes, Lieutenant. I have only this flannel waistcoat to finish. I have put everything to dry in the cupboard behind the chimney-piece in the house."

The house! He means the one that sheltered us last night. It resembles that in which we slept on the night of September 25th; it resembles all the other houses in the village; only certainly it ranks among the least dirty of them. In my frenzy of organization and cleansing I have had the greasy dishes washed which littered the chairs and the bed; I have scraped the stained table with a piece of glass; not even the kneading-trough have I forgotten. Moreover, I have put back the faded family photographs I found lying about in confusion; closed all the yawning drawers, and arranged in the linen-chest coarse shirts and wearing apparel, a riding coat, a green dress, and some chintzes. Pannechon has hung a cloth before the window, so that I am no longer compelled to look on empty window-frames and the shell-holes desolating the meadows.

Now that the door is closed and I am alone with him and Viollet, a taciturn and devoted lad, I no longer feel the depression which always overwhelms me at the sight of the desolated and shattered homes. This one, for the time being at least, is barred against the intrusion of passers-by. Peace has descended upon it; I do not want that peace to be disturbed. If anyone comes prying and poking his nose around the door, he will quickly find himself in the road again.

Sitting before the table smoking my pipe, I am writing and making notes of events worthy of remembrance. My pen runs well; my pipe draws well. From time to time the distant sound of guns makes the walls tremble and blows our impromptu curtain into the room. That troubles me but little, however; it signifies nothing to me. On the other hand, the crackling of the wood burning in the grate fascinates me and holds my attention. I love this song of the fire and the dancing of the flames. Pannechon and Viollet are sitting opposite each other beside the fireplace; Pannechon, with swollen cheeks, is blowing with all the force of his lungs through a long metal tube which branches at the end in the form of a lyre; his efforts send the glowing sparks up the chimney. Viollet is carefully covering some onions with hot cinders. The day is dying. The solid things about us grow more and more shadowy as twilight descends. The guns fall silent. It almost seems to me that the pendulum of the clock on the mantelshelf is going to start again, steadily and rhythmically marking the flight of the minutes.

All at once Pannechon jumps to his feet so violently that he overturns his chair. He rushes to the next room shouting:

"Fire! Fire! There's a fire!"

We run out, bumping against each other, to the door. A stifling smoke envelops us. We choke, we cough, we weep.

"The pump, the pump! There's a camp bucket here! . . ."

The pump creaks; the bucket fills; a steady stream is directed on the flames. Smoke swirls up in dense, choking clouds; we cough so violently that we almost vomit.

"The door! Shut the door!"

What idiot has just come in? There came a violent gust of air at the very moment when we were getting the fire under.

"Hullo! "says a voice. "What's all this about? You're making a bit of a hullabaloo, aren't you?"

It is Porchon.

"Come along, old man," I cry. "You must help if you wish to sleep here tonight. Pump, pump—like the devil!"

And the four of us fly about as madly as devils in holy water. The pump nearly bursts itself; we wallow in a black flood and tread on each other's toes; but little by little the clouds of smoke die away, the air becomes breathable, our eyes cease to run.

"Bring the candle from that table," I say to Pannechon, "and let's have a look at the damage."

The inquiry is short. There is no stone-work behind the chimney-piece. One side of it formed the back of a cupboard with wooden doors, which was used for drying linen. The side had cracked and the flames had got through and set fire to the cupboard doors.

What about the linen inside? Has the worst happened?

"Pannechon, our linen?"

Pannechon smiles, Pannechon is well pleased with himself.

"Ah! Lieutenant, I'm a smart fellow. I had just got it away when the fire broke out. It was all aired—ah, no, there was an old pair of socks which were still wet, so I left them. Yes, there they are—socks no longer, but cinders! It must have been those that smothered us, together with a bundle of rags left at the bottom."

So everything is all right then. Porchon approaches the bed and caresses the eiderdown.

"Ah! old friend, but that was a narrow escape," he says affection-ately. "You shall wrap us up snugly shortly." Then raising his voice, he addresses me: "Come along, it is time to mess. Do not forget that I bought some pork yesterday evening from that old man back in the valley. There are also some apple fritters, and still one more of Presle's famous fowls."

Saturday, October 3rd.

Letters at last! Forty letters at once! And the postman tells me there are still others to follow! I plunge into the mass. I read voraciously, until I am a being intoxicated. I take them from the heap, just as they come to hand, slit the envelope open with my finger, and absorb the contents of the whole letter at once. How short a time it takes, after all, to read forty letters!

Then I re-read them slowly, line by line, as one sips an exquisite liqueur of whose bouquet one's palate never tires. My letters no longer swamp me; I select now, guided by a sure instinct.

And of all those letters, I preserve a few only—those each separate word of which bears a message of hope and encouragement for me. They are the more intimate, hopeful, brighter ones; they are the letters for which I have looked so long in vain. Having read and re-read them, I place them where, at any moment, in any place, they will be available. Meanwhile, because of them and through them, I have become more confident of myself. . . .

Since the dawn, we have been in a steep-sided ravine, whose fresh green is most refreshing to the eyes. The guns are firing irregularly. A German battery is shelling some position out of sight; the shells fly over us at a great height, singing queerly and accompanied by the usual rustling of a heavy object flying through the air.

The older and seasoned soldiers laugh constantly while they banter and twit some new recruits who have just rejoined the colours, and who, each time a shell sails past, search the sky with anxious eyes, seeking to follow its course.

"Don't let them worry you, my boy! They are only rubbish!"

"They never explode, those big shells, as you will see for yourself. At least, that's what we have been told."

"Ah, *là là!* Are you sure? . . ."

"You shut up and leave them alone! You want to try and make them believe that they do explode, perhaps. Don't believe them! They are only trying to frighten you!"

Another man good-naturedly adds:

"I shouldn't take any notice of what they say. One says this; another that! Let them go on talking and wait and see for yourselves. You won't have long to wait!"

A true prophecy that, for we leave for the advance posts in the woods. The march is a pleasant one. We are not shelled; what rifle fire there is, is far away; we hear the crackling distinctly, but no bullets go humming past us. We march along in single file by one of those damp tracks where the sunlight, streaming through the leaves, takes to itself a greenish hue. Porchon is busy amusing himself by letting small branches fly back at me as he moves onwards. With a jump I place myself alongside him and so stop his little game.

"Have you seen the Captain of the 8th?" I ask him. "He has come back with his cheek still in bandages. His wound cannot be properly healed yet."

"Yes, I have seen him! He certainly doesn't make a fuss about his wounds!"

"What do you think of the new men? . . . Do they impress you well?"

"Er . . . yes! . . . Oh, yes!"

Porchon's tone is doubtful; he appears to be rather preoccupied.

"What is wrong with them?" I ask. "I can only speak for my own section of course; but they have at least sent me two corporals and a sergeant who seem to me sound, well-meaning sort of fellows."

"Well-meaning enough, I grant you. You can always expect that. But it is true I am rather worried. You see, the new contingents seem to be comprised of nothing but non-coms., sergeants and corporals. What's the good of them? However hard you try, you can't be everywhere at the same time. Of course, while you are looking after your right, the left, unsupported, gives way. . . . I am sorry indeed Roux has been sent to hospital!"

"What! The Adjutant in hospital?"

"Yes! The day before yesterday. He'll be out of harness for some time. A good section leader lost!"

Two cannon shots, thundering out almost simultaneously, impel us to look up quickly.

Those shells were not 75's or 105's. And where are the guns? They seemed to be under our very noses, yet they are not to be seen. Thirty yards away some gunners are coming and going, busying themselves with some business whose nature it is difficult to grasp at a glance. We approach them and, suddenly, almost at our feet, we see the guns, admirably hidden beneath a pile of brushwood, with a palisade of branches all round. An artificial thicket is the result, capable of deceiving the eye ten paces away.

"Oh, that's something like!" I exclaim. "It is an artistic triumph. I am going to congratulate the gunners."

The moment, however, I get near the guns, and slightly in front of them, a deafening, stunning explosion takes place. The rush of air almost knocks me over; my head seems to have been shattered and my ears tingle painfully. A gunner laughingly calls out to me:

"Hallo, Lieutenant! Have you heard our 90's yet?"

So these are the 90's! One of my men growls bitterly:

"What idiocy! To put these mechanics here with their two machines simply to make a noise! They would have something better to think about than making us jump if they had to go and do some fighting!"

We are in the heart of the wood. We scale a slope and descend the further side. Everyone is silent, a prey to that instinctive feeling which proximity to the Boches causes. It can hardly be described as uneasiness; rather is it a complex sensation which compels action even before the impulse behind it has formed in the mind. One instinctively walks on tiptoe, holds one's bayonet to prevent it rattling, suppresses a cough. It is as if someone had said: "Be careful! I can smell the Germans!" There are, of course, some men who do not feel this sensation as keenly as others, but the soldier who is a complete stranger to it is a rarity; time only quickens it, and with some it is an unfailing indication of the enemy's presence.

How thick these woods are! Beneath the giant trees whose lower branches begin to spread at least sixty feet above the earth, the exuberant undergrowth runs riot. It stretches across and over the path in wonderful confusion, branches twining with branches, until they seem designedly to have combined to check our progress. Thick and flexible, we have to thrust them aside with our hands before we can go on; while tenacious offshoots, wrapping themselves about our legs, send us stumbling constantly.

To right and left are green depths, as far as the eye can reach. Green, too, is the moss, fresh and velvety in the shadows; tinged with russet and gold where the sun has caught it. Green are the trunks of the age-old trees, with the humid, unhealthy greenness which betokens rot; green the countless leaves, changing and varying with the caprice of the breeze; green, yet gold-flecked, are the leaves already touched by autumn's finger.

I raise my head while we march along, seeking the sky's limpid blue for relief; but I can see only a few patches of the heavens, tranquil and serene above the restless quivering of the woods, which lighten the way for us, prisoners of this prodigious multitude of trees, of this unpitying sea of undergrowth.

We have almost fallen into the trenches, which open unexpectedly at our feet. The heads of men appear above the soil; then the men hoist themselves out of the deep cutting with the aid of their rifles, and the relief is effected, very swiftly and without noise, in broad daylight.

These trenches are splendid, deeply sunk in the chalk, with low parapets supported by wattles. Above them, a roof of leaves droops almost down to the parapet, leaving only a narrow opening through which we can survey the terrain, without being seen. It is not possible to see far, because the visible field of fire extends only eighteen feet or so beyond our rifles, thirty feet at the most at the widest part. This zone, too, is covered with the stumps of felled trees. Beyond it there are more, as dense as those behind us, and therefore more redoubtable than the Germans they hide.

The terrain slopes steeply away from us for a hundred yards or so, then rises again to a summit, which marks the horizon a mile away. The side of this rising is covered with undergrowth and, here and there, high trees. The sinking sun bathes the wood in a crimson light, which ruddies the leaves on the higher branches of the trees. And while the pungent odour of the woods rather oppresses me, my eyes weary not, until the darkness of the night extinguishes the colours, of contemplating the trees, which seem to touch the sky, whose leaves tremble in the failing light and which appear beautiful beyond description on this fading autumnal day.

Sunday, October 4th.

Porchon has reassured himself. While we sit, plunging our pocket-knives in the same tin of beef, he enunciates considerations which have tended to induce this happy frame of mind.

"When we arrived here yesterday, I don't mind confessing that the place gave me a cold shiver up the spine. It appeared to me a cut-throat sort of hole, this little corner. However, I have reconnoitred the ground, and on my return I have found myself as comfy as formerly I had been disturbed. Have you tried to walk through the thicket over there?"

"Yes."

"Did you get far?"

"I gave it up after advancing a few steps."

"Naturally. I, too, attempted it, and, like you, decided it Was better to abandon it. Under the circumstances, then, there seemed nothing for me to do but to obey the advice I received when we arrived—to guard the clearings and send out patrols from time to time. A very nice type, the lieutenant who was in command here! He saw me raiding his cigarette-papers, and in a flash offered me the book. 'You want some? Take those, then.' It is a long time since I have been so well off. . . . . Ah, well! What do you wish for most? I only hope we have a night as calm as that of yesterday, a day of fine weather such as this, and return to our quarters for dinner—

The valley of my dream where I sleep in a bed.

"You notice, old man, I possess some genius for improvisation! Meanwhile, however, my bit of foresight should carry us on comfortably until the 8th. After that, who knows? But it is at least something to be grateful for to have four days before one."

"Touch wood!" I say. "Touch wood! We are not back in the valley yet, nor in our beds."

A quartermaster coming up at this moment interrupts us. It appears that one of us two must go to the battalion headquarters to receive instructions. I set out, the messenger acting as guide.

The major's dugout is situated near a fairly wide cross road. A forest alley prolongs to right and left a level perspective; the sun, which at this hour is directly overhead, appears as a magnificent avenue cutting right through the heart of the forest. The company in reserve is stationed here, but not a man is visible in the sunlight. When one gets nearer, however, heads pop up out of a trench among the brambles which cover it. In some astonishment, I ask myself what inconceivable folly has led these men to hide themselves in their trench on such a day, and why they watch me passing with such astonishment in their eyes.

I encounter several old comrades at the entrance of the hut in which the captain is lying sick. It appears that an attack by the Boches is anticipated. Consequently, certain dispositions must be arranged before nightfall. I take down all instructions in my note-book, and after a few words of general advice we each depart in our respective directions.

I was approaching our trenches, walking musingly through the clearing, watching the splashes of sunlight playing over the moss, when a strange sound impelled me to halt transfixed. The sound took the form of light, aerial music, as silvery and as transparent as the sky which carried its waves to me. That welcome music had wings; it went high, higher even than the great trees, higher than the trilling of the lark. There were instants when it seemed to draw far away, being heard then only with difficulty; then it recovered force and sounded clear and distinct though limpid and immaterial. A breath of wind shook the leaves and brought a flood of the melody down to me, before it was dispersed far and wide.

It was the voice of bells in some village church.

I stood there, unmoving, listening to this chant of the bells wafting through the woods, where night and day men faced one another, seeking to kill each other.

Their message was not sad. From the heights of the heavens wherein it resounds it spreads widely over earth and men alike. The Germans in their trenches hear it, as we hear it, but the bells speak not to them as they speak to us.

To us they say:

"Hope, sons of France! I am near you, the voice of all the firesides you have left behind. To each one of you I bring a vision of that corner of the earth where the heart remains. Confidence be with you forever, sons of France, confidence and strength for ever. I sing the life immortal of the Fatherland."

To them they say:

"Madmen who believed that France could die! Hear me! Above the little church, whose stained-glass windows lie in fragments on the pavements, the belfry still stands. It is the belfry that sends me to you, laughing and mocking. Through me it is the village that defies you. I see. . . . I see . . . whatever you have done, I see. Whatever you may do, I shall see. I am not afraid of you. Because I know that the day will come when the cock on the steeple, staring unflinchingly towards the far horizon, will see you in desperate flight, while the innumerable bodies of your slain shall lie thick over the land!"

Night. Letters have been brought to me. One of the envelopes contains sorrow for me. I have learnt that a friend is dead.

And I welcome the darkness. Its blackness cannot be too black for me; I have even hidden myself at the bottom of the trench, because a diffused light wanders amid the boles of the age-old trees before it; and Welcome also is the silence of night. Near me an occasional furtive movement reveals the presence of men who are watching. Nothing else. Not even firing in the far distance. I open my eyes in the blackness and see again the living face of my friend, frank, eyes clear and loyal, mouth slightly disdainful, beneath a closely-clipped moustache.

The news has shocked me greatly. A torpor steals over me; the blood beats violently in my temples; I am fevered. And suddenly I hear a murmur, very low, very far away, indefinable. Am I dreaming? Two soldiers, perhaps, gossiping somewhere close at hand. Yes, they are the voices of men I hear, but now they are silent. My head is burning, and still the blood thunders in my temples without a pause. Then the murmur recommences, the same as it was before. It increases; someone is speaking. I cannot distinguish the words, yet the voice is familiar to me: I know it well. But how distant it is! It seems to resound far away in space, beyond the reach of my senses; it rises from obscure depths within me; it awakens in me what is most intimate in the dead past! Low and soft, it is the voice of my friend!

"Lieutenant!"

That is a raucous voice which causes me to raise my head.

"Lieutenant!—Lieutenant!"

"What's the matter?"

"You hear that firing away to the left?"

Firing!—Firing! It is true; the woods; the night; the advance posts; the attack that was anticipated. . . . A few stars shine between the trees; it is very cold; a branch creaks, while somewhere away to our left resounds a prolonged and continuous crackling, which echoes from one end of the ravine to the other. Can they be fighting further away down the line? Is this the attack?

I leave the trench and walk slowly from one end of the line to the other. My men are standing at attention, their rifles resting on the parapet; the non-coms, are in their places; we are ready. Gropingly I enter the narrow passageway opening into the undergrowth away in front and beyond our trenches. At the end of this, the clearing starts. I count my steps, eight, nine, ten; here is a giant beech, marking the entrance. Little by little my eyes grow accustomed to the darkness. I walk forward more confidently, almost quickly. I should have arrived at my destination by now. Three times I whistle cautiously, three times a whistle rings out in reply, and at the same time a fugitive ray of light gleams on a bayonet in the clearing and I can make out a dark figure. The sentries are keeping good guard!

"Nothing before you, Chabeau?"

"Nothing, Lieutenant!"

"Who is with you?"

"Gilon."

"That's all right. Keep your eyes and your ears open, but do not start firing if only a leaf rustles. Remember there is wire before you to which we have fastened empty meat-tins with a few pebbles inside. A Boche has only to touch the wire to set up a deuce of a rattle. Also, do not fire if you should hear crackers going off to the right or left. Just guard your particular corner to the very best of your ability. Understand?"

"I understand. Lieutenant." I am just going to leave him, when a gun fires a little behind us, not twenty yards away; we saw a flame spurt out of the muzzle. A moment later there is a second report; then the thunder of a squall, and bullets rush and whistle a short distance away.

"Lieutenant? You heard?"

A cry has vibrated through the night, coming from far away to the right, and as if it had been intended for us alone, it echoes and re-echoes through the trees around us, with poignant, tragic force.

"To arms!"

A glimpse of light, quickly extinguished, passes from one end of the French trenches to the other. A crisp outbreak rends the darkness; branches, bullet-shattered, fall to the earth. We have flung ourselves flat, face downwards. Fortunately our men are firing high; the slope of the earth saves us. Still lying flat, we crawl with difficulty through an entanglement of brambles. Chabeau and Gilon are so close to me that I can hear their laboured breathing. Often a whining bullet grazes us; but most of them fly above us right across the hollow, to embed themselves in the further side.

"We had better shout out. Lieutenant," Chabeau suggests.

"No, no! Follow me!"

I recollect that between two stretches of trenches there remains an unexcavated interval, and it is towards that spot I set my crawling course, followed by my two men. I peer into the darkness intently, and gradually my eyes acquire an amazing keenness. Jets of rifle fire serve to guide me. They flash out constantly on the same line, in the middle of which there remains a patch of darkness. We are directly opposite that patch, which represents our haven. More bullets sing and whine about us, falling harmlessly to either side. Chabeau, with his mouth close to my ear, says:

"I think we are all right now Lieutenant, but we have had a warm time, haven't we?"

"Rather!" I reply. "And it is not yet finished. Some terrified idiot may still serve us dirtily, when he sees us coming from the same direction as the Boches!"

The two echo in chorus:

"Ah, yes! . . . Ah, yes! . . . It is possible! . . ."

"Wait for me here without moving an inch," I command. "I am going forward alone to try and rejoin the men. When I have warned them, I will return for you."

I rise deliberately and dash with all speed across the open space separating me from the trenches. How easy it was! The noise of the rifles changes abruptly; when I sprang to my feet, the firing sounded harsh, almost sharp; now the voice of the bullets is deadened and dulled. A few leaps suffice to carry me well to the rear of the trenches. But how of those two others, lying flat on their faces in the open? Each second is of urgent importance.

"Lieutenant!—Lieutenant!—who is there?" A big man rushes up to me, stares through the darkness into my face, and then:

"Ah! So it is you, Lieutenant! But that lifts a weight off my heart! You are not hurt? I told myself that you could not be wounded. I knew you had gone out; I held up my fire and no one about me fired, and we were directly in front of the cutting. But, name of a dog! how the time dragged!"

The man who addresses me in this way is Souesme, one of my sergeants. This is my opportunity.

"Listen to me, Souesme. Gilon and Chabeau are still out there before the trenches. I am going out to fetch them in. Meanwhile, you remain here and wait for us."

A few moments later I am safely back again among my men, accompanied by the two men and the sergeant. It is as Souesme affirmed. My men on the right, where the sergeant was stationed, have not fired a shot. Still further to the right, however, in the neighbouring trench, the spitting of the rifles does not cease for a second. The fusillade, disordered, breathless, betrays the anxiety of the men. And my half section to the left is creating a similar ridiculous din.

The Germans are replying vigorously, but their efforts are just as wild and valueless as our own. Almost all the bullets fly high over us towards the top of the slope behind us. They must be falling much more thickly among the company in reserve than they are here. Only every now and again does a stray shot tatter the leaves which form the roof of our trench or send up the pebbles before our eyes.

As speedily as possible, I get among the men composing the left wing of my section. They are still firing madly and blindly. I roughly shake one or two of them and command volley fire. They obey me. And at each word of command others imitate their example, while the resulting volley increases and my voice carries further and further. In this way, I gradually regain grip of my men. Then, with them well in hand, I let one more volley go, before shouting the "Cease fire!" The word passes from man to man right along the line, and peace descends on my trench. The example seems contagious. In the trenches right and left a similar command rings out and silence descends.

The Boches also put a term to their fusillade Two or three bullets still fly amid the trees, fired from one knows not where, but that is all.

The smoke clears away, enabling us to see more or less distinctly. To our fevered imaginations the underwood before the trenches appears now to be less distant than earlier in the night; we think, too, we can detect dark forms coming and going amidst it.

The silence endures—a silence so intense as to seem almost palpable. It swallows us as the floodgates of a mill-pool engulf the waters. I strain my ears to catch the slightest sound. The woods, lashed no longer by the frenzy and fury of man, regain their usual mystery. Breezes almost imperceptibly rustle the leaves and set the shoots of the brambles swaying; a little round living thing appears suddenly on top of the parapet, glides to a corner of the trench, climbs a stake and vanishes amid the leaves which form our roof—a field-mouse searching for scraps!

From time to time the breeze momentarily increases, until the whole of the woods are alive with rustlings and tremblings. It comes from the north behind us, and is bitterly cold and biting; then it passes onwards, awakening the trees from their slumber right up to the hilltop. We feel like lost souls, surrounded by a thousand hidden menaces, so weak and fearful that the advent of real danger would surely find us unarmed against it! Some prowling night beast moves in the thicket.

"There are Boches there right enough!" a man exclaims.

"They must be plotting some pretty mischief seeing how quiet they keep," adds a second. "They are stealing up one by one, and when there is a sufficient number of them, they'll rush down on top of us in a flash. We shall be done for!"

Another man seizes my arm impulsively and says in a low tone:

"There are two of them there—quite close—behind that bush. I can see them right enough! They have helmets; they are standing close to one another. Oh, Lieutenant, we must fire!"

I am about to reply when someone moves behind me. A man is bending down towards the trench calling:

"Lieutenant! Lieutenant!"

"I am here. What do you want?"

"Ah, Lieutenant, you will have to remain all night. The wood is full of Boches. From our side, we can see them hiding not ten yards away. We must fire. . . ."

"No, return to your place instantly! I forbid you to fire, do you understand? You will fire only when I give the word."

But still another man approaches me. I recognize him as Boulier, one of my best men, a stolid, cool-headed peasant, who has been fighting since the first day of the war. He jumps down to the trench beside me and says in a calm voice:

"Lieutenant, I have marked two Boches spying upon us. They are hidden behind that big beech at the entrance to the cutting over there. There are hundreds and thousands of them a little further back. In a moment or two they will charge. But the two of whom I tell you—it is certain they are there. Look for yourself!"

Despite myself, I look. Boulier continues in a babble:

"Behind the beech, nowhere else. One is taller than the other, or else one of them must be stooping. Every now and again the big one bends forward, as if stretching his neck to look about. The other keeps still. Ah, the scum!...."

Intently I watch the beech tree pointed out by Boulier. What he affirms is true, perhaps. I listen calmly to all he has to say, his face so close that I can feel his warm breath on mine:

"There, the other has moved a little; the big one wants to speak to him. He is stooping down. Good! There you are, he is rising again. Ah, the camels!"

Peering so constantly into the blackness wearies my eyes. Lights begin to dance before them; rings of flame begin to whirl vertiginously. I close my eyes for a moment. And when I open them again, I can see behind the beech two unmoving human beings, bending low in a listening attitude. I shake myself, look at my hands, at the wattles supporting the parapet, and then once more at the beech. I can see nothing now but beeches and leaves.

"There are no Boches there," I tell Boulier. "You also have lost your head."

I jump up over the front of the trench. The man calls me back.

"Lieutenant! Lieutenant! Don't go! You are going to get yourself hurt! ..."

At the first step I stumble over the stump of a tree and almost fall. When I have regained my balance, I can see the two Germans behind the tree again. And on the instant I detect them, a conviction seizes me that they too have seen me. A storm of fear assails me. My heart seems to become empty of blood; my flesh grows icy cold and trembles violently. In desperation I get grip of myself, fighting back an impulse to

167

cry out aloud or to take to my heels; the effort of will causes my nails to enter my palms.

Drawing my revolver, I continue to advance. Instead, however, of moving without haste in complete self-possession, I rush blindly and furiously towards the right.

Suddenly I find myself amid the undergrowth and stop. Turning, I find the beech immediately behind me so close that its roots protrude from the earth at my feet. I run fingers up and down the bark, stamp on the very spot where I thought I had seen the two Boches; I push on into the clearing, beating the bushes to right and left. I find nothing, nothing at all. And I the leader of those men, I to whom that night had been confided a portion of the front behind which lay France and its well-being, I had almost abandoned myself to a lunatic's frenzy. Panic had made of me a brute among brutes. I was grateful now for the darkness, which veiled me and my actions from the eyes of my soldiers. When I returned to the trench Boulier on the parapet extended his hand towards me. I jumped down beside him. I had nothing to say to him.

A few minutes later a volley bursts out from the opposite lines, to which our men reply, and the fusillade starts again.

This time the Boches fire lower. Every instant bullets bury themselves in the earth about us, striking sharply. I hear one of my corporals swear when a bullet smashes the upper part of his arm. I am master of myself again now. No longer are my senses subject to illusion; lucidly, one after the other, I check my impressions; all my confidence returns to me.

Above all can I hear the crackling of the enemy's rifles. They sound sharply, exactly opposite us; but the bullets seem to come from a great distance, which serves to thin them out. I recall Vauxmarie, the firing at thirty yards, then at ten, then at point-blank range. The present fusillade is not like that, and I feel sure that up to the present the Germans have not yet left their trenches. More than that, I feel convinced they will not leave them. On the other side of the ravine, taking cover in a trench similar to ours, behind a similar breastwork, they, too, tremble at every rustling of the leaves. The night was the same for all men in the wood; like ourselves, the Boches were afraid.

A star shell rises high in the sky and bursts into startling resplendency; so strong was the light with which it flooded the earth that the shadow of each branch, of each leaf, was projected in minute perfection of detail upon the whitened surface of the parapet, on our faces, on our hands.

The star streamed through the heavens until a gust of wind made it waver; then it commenced to descend slowly and leisurely until finally dying from sight. And then the darkness was more impenetrable than ever.

The fusillade had burst out from the enemy's trenches more violently than ever the moment the wan, pale light of the star irradiated the earth. Now the darkness has again descended, the firing does not decrease. Rather the whistling of bullets increases. Other star shells rise and burst; on each occasion I see the rank of my men, one pressing against the other, necks extended, watching closely the course of the star.

A bullet strikes a metal object behind me, doubtless some old water-flask. The sound brings me to attention again. I listen to the bullets, their whining, the dead thud they make against the trunks of the trees, the lash-like hissing they make when flying far towards the trenches of the reserve, the long-drawn, the musical note of those flying still higher and passing over the hilltop into space.

The steps of someone approaching are heard. Someone is coming, walking evenly and steadily, through the mortal hail. I see the man is erect; he is following the line of the trenches; from time to time he halts and bends a little, as though to speak to those in the trench, well sheltered from the shots. Then he rises and, quite erect, continues on his way, thrusting aside the brambles with a stick in his hand. In this way, with the same appearance of indifference and nonchalance, he passes through the leaden tempest raging about the terrain which separates us from the neighbouring trench. A few yards from me he seems to hesitate, moves back a little while looking about him, then in a low voice he calls my name.

"I am here," I say. "Can you hear me? Come towards my voice."

And Porchon, seating himself tranquilly on the parapet, his legs in the trench, his head and body exposed to the bullets, offers me his hand, saying:

"Good evening, old man."

And there he remains, joking and laughing and jeering at the fears of the men, which had not abated since sunset.

"You know Timmie, the deaf man, he saw about four hundred Germans in a heap. I took him by the arm and dragged him over towards the wood. He fought like a man possessed. I had to release him at last, as he would have screamed. And so I went forward all alone; and this cursed Timmie said—yes, my boy, he said: 'Oh! Lieutenant, God permits you to walk over there!'"

He lowered his voice to tell me that one of the sentries had been wounded by his comrades when the firing just started. He commenced to laugh again, relating how a sergeant, seeing him walking along the parapet when the firing was heaviest, began to call himself indescribable things, jumped out of the trench and swore he would remain outside until daybreak, and only after enormous trouble and threats of punishment had Porchon induced him to get down again with his men. He further confided in me that he was rather perturbed at the shortage of cartridges and that he had dispatched a messenger to the commander for a further supply.

"I should not fire unless it becomes absolutely urgent," he said. "A strong Boche patrol entered the ravine a short time ago, when the star shells went up. I know it has returned now. Butel has been to see. They won't budge again tonight. This firing means nothing. Let it pass."

With a quick jump he came to his feet again.

"Listen to me," I cried. "I am going with you."

He refused decidedly. "No, no! Your place is here. You must remain."

I watched him move away towards the left, halt several times again and seat himself to talk more easily. As soon as the men saw him they said to one another:

"It is Lieutenant Porchon."

In this way his progress is announced, causing calmness and confidence right along the line.

At last he returns and jumps down into the trench between Boulier and myself.

"Ouf!" he exclaimed, "but things were looking rather nasty with us. I believe I was right in making my little tour. Half-past two in the morning; time is drawing on. All will go well now until daylight."

Boulier suddenly exclaimed:

"All the same. Lieutenant, it is not an ordinary thing that you have done. There were a thousand chances of your being wounded. And that would have been my fault, the fault of we good-for-nothings. Yes, it would have been our fault—don't let us talk about it!"

"To every man his business," replied Porchon. "If I had been you. Boulier, I would not have risked my skin as I have done. Just reflect a little, and you will understand."

Then, laughing still that laugh of a twenty year-old boy, he taps me on the shoulder and says:

"Today is the 5th, the day of our relief. Unless I am very much mistaken we shall sleep tonight in our beds. Goodbye for the moment. I am going back to my men."

Boulier, near me, his elbows on the parapet, watched him vanish amid the shadows. And he repeated to himself softly and without ceasing:

"Ah! what a man! . . . What a man! Heavens! . . . What a man!"

An intense emotion seemed to grip him by the throat, and the feeling in his voice shows that he is stirred to the heart's depth.

"Ah! What a man! . . . What a man!"

And that was all he could say.

Monday, October 5th,

Porchon brings me some news. When the quartermaster came to announce that the relief would take place this evening, he confided in him that we were going to change our position. Porchon hums gaily:

We go no more to the woods,
For we have dined!

"You will perceive," he cries, "that my latest effort as an improviser is more conspicuous than ever. Those words do none the less adequately express my meaning because they were sung. The woods bore one; they suffocate one; one can see nothing; soon now we shall have a plain before us. Tell me what you will think on finding yourself perched on the side of a hill, with the summit, which you must take, whatever the cost, before your eyes? It will be exciting at least! And then it is so clear and distinct. One understands what is required of one. Ah! but we're going to have gay days over there: days of saps, of mine warfare, of assaults."

"Is it far from here?" I ask.

"Not very far. A few miles away to the east. It is just before the heights, a snug little corner in a valley. I love its name, because it has such a clear and open sound. Positively, it will give one real pleasure to fight in such a place."

"And this name?" I ask.

"Eparges!"

LEONAUR

ALSO FROM LEONAUR
AVAILABLE IN SOFTCOVER OR HARDCOVER WITH DUST JACKET

FARAWAY CAMPAIGN *by F. James*—Experiences of an Indian Army Cavalry Officer in Persia & Russia During the Great War.

REVOLT IN THE DESERT *by T. E. Lawrence*—An account of the experiences of one remarkable British officer's war from his own perspective.

MACHINE-GUN SQUADRON *by A. M. G.*—The 20th Machine Gunners from British Yeomanry Regiments in the Middle East Campaign of the First World War.

A GUNNER'S CRUSADE *by Antony Bluett*—The Campaign in the Desert, Palestine & Syria as Experienced by the Honourable Artillery Company During the Great War .

DESPATCH RIDER *by W. H. L. Watson*—The Experiences of a British Army Motorcycle Despatch Rider During the Opening Battles of the Great War in Europe.

TIGERS ALONG THE TIGRIS *by E. J. Thompson*—The Leicestershire Regiment in Mesopotamia During the First World War.

HEARTS & DRAGONS *by Charles R. M. F. Crutwell*—The 4th Royal Berkshire Regiment in France and Italy During the Great War, 1914-1918.

INFANTRY BRIGADE: 1914 *by John Ward*—The Diary of a Commander of the 15th Infantry Brigade, 5th Division, British Army, During the Retreat from Mons.

DOING OUR 'BIT' *by Ian Hay*—Two Classic Accounts of the Men of Kitchener's 'New Army' During the Great War including *The First 100,000 & All In It.*

AN EYE IN THE STORM *by Arthur Ruhl*—An American War Correspondent's Experiences of the First World War from the Western Front to Gallipoli-and Beyond.

STAND & FALL *by Joe Cassells*—With the Middlesex Regiment Against the Bolsheviks 1918-19.

RIFLEMAN MACGILL'S WAR *by Patrick MacGill*—A Soldier of the London Irish During the Great War in Europe including *The Amateur Army, The Red Horizon & The Great Push.*

WITH THE GUNS *by C. A. Rose & Hugh Dalton*—Two First Hand Accounts of British Gunners at War in Europe During World War 1- Three Years in France with the Guns and With the British Guns in Italy.

THE BUSH WAR DOCTOR *by Robert V. Dolbey*—The Experiences of a British Army Doctor During the East African Campaign of the First World War.

CPSIA information can be obtained at www.ICGtesting.com
Printed in the USA
LVOW08s2145121113

361035LV00001B/110/P